Supervising Food Safety
(Level 3)

A text for Level 3 Food Safety courses
and a reference for supervisors

Ideal for use on LEVEL 3 RIPH • CIEH • REHIS Accredited Courses

**Richard A. Sprenger,
BSc(Hons), DMS, FCIEH, MREHIS, FSOFHT**

Managing Director   Highfield.co.uk Limited

First published October 1999
Reprinted 2000, 2001, 2002, 2003, 2004, 2005, 2006
10th Edition 2007

PUBLISHED BY
©**HIGHFIELD.CO.UK LIMITED**

Highfield House, Sidings Court, Lakeside, Doncaster, South Yorkshire, DN4 5NL, UK
Tel: +44 0845 2260350   Facsimile: +44 0845 2260360
E-mail: richard@highfield.co.uk

Websites: www.highfield.co.uk   www.foodsafetytrainers.co.uk

ISBN 1-904544-78-9

Printed by Trafford Press • Telephone: 01302 367509

All rights reserved. No part of this publication may be reproduced, stored in a retrieval system, or transmitted in any form or by any means, electronic, photocopying, recording or otherwise, without the prior permission of Highfield.co.uk ltd.

Contents

SUPERVISING FOOD SAFETY (LEVEL 3)

Preface...3

Chapter 1   An introduction to food safety...4

Chapter 2   Microbiology..8

Chapter 3   Food contamination and its prevention...14

Chapter 4   Food poisoning and foodborne disease...27

Chapter 5   Personal hygiene...43

Chapter 6   The storage & temperature control of food...50

Chapter 7   Food spoilage & preservation...67

Chapter 8   The design & construction of food premises & equipment.......................76

Chapter 9   Cleaning & disinfection..89

Chapter 10   Pest control...98

Chapter 11   Supervisory management..111

Chapter 12   Food safety legislation...135

Glossary...150

Index..153

Preface

The prevention of most food poisoning outbreaks is relatively simple and well understood. Cook food thoroughly, protect it from contamination and keep it cold or hot.

But despite our knowledge of these simple controls and the millions of first-tier food handlers who have attended food hygiene courses, the number of cases of food poisoning remains at an unacceptable level. Attendance on food hygiene courses alone, even when obtaining certificates, appears to have had little effect. It could be argued that on-the-job training to promote competency, and effective instruction, motivation, supervision and control are an even more important part of the overall strategy necessary to significantly reduce levels of foodborne illness and food complaints. In other words, knowledgeable and competent supervisors and managers are the key to food safety.

I have written this book with the intention of providing supervisors and middle managers with the essential, practical information to enable them to manage staff to provide safe food. *Supervising Food Safety (Level 3)* is based on the syllabuses of the Level 3 Food Safety Courses provided by the Chartered Institute of Environmental Health, the Royal Environmental Health Institute of Scotland, the Royal Institute of Public Health and the Royal Society for the Promotion of Health.

In addition to assisting candidates to successfully complete the above courses, *Supervising Food Safety (Level 3)* should be used as a reference to help supervisors make correct decisions with regard to food safety. Emphasis has been placed on the measures necessary to control the most common reasons for food poisoning outbreaks, including temperature control, effective cooling, storage and thawing, preventing contamination and the destruction of food poisoning bacteria.

Many of the food scares relating to, for example, salmonella in eggs, *E. coli* O157, listeria and high levels of food poisoning would probably not have occurred if the highest standards of hygiene had been observed and the recommendations in this book had been followed.

If you rigorously apply the principles of food safety detailed throughout *Supervising Food Safety (Level 3)*, you should avoid your food business becoming one of the food poisoning statistics or, even worse, starting off the next food scare.

1 An introduction to food safety

Safe food is food which is free of contaminants and will not cause illness or harm. Persons involved in food poisoning investigations often remark about the cleanliness of the premises responsible. If food hygiene is intended to ensure the safety of food and prevent food poisoning then it follows that hygiene is more than cleanliness: it involves all measures necessary to ensure the safety and wholesomeness of food during preparation, processing, manufacture, storage, transportation, distribution, handling, sale and supply. This involves:

- protecting food from risk of contamination, i.e. preventing objectionable matter getting into food, including harmful bacteria, poisons and foreign bodies;
- preventing any bacteria present multiplying to a level which would result in illness of consumers or the early spoilage of food;
- destroying any harmful bacteria in the food by thorough cooking, processing or irradiation; and
- discarding unfit or contaminated food.

The cost of poor hygiene and food poisoning

Persons carrying on a food business have legal, commercial and moral obligations to provide safe food. The costs resulting from food poisoning can be very high, as are those from poor hygiene. These costs, both financial and social, fall on employers and employees as well as those persons who are ill. Costs for employers include:

- the loss of working days, and productivity, from illness caused by employees eating contaminated food;
- the closure of food premises, or the prohibition of processes by local authority action;
- brand damage: a loss of business and reputation, either from bad publicity or from public reaction to poor standards, food poisoning outbreaks and even deaths;
- increased risk of pest infestation;
- fines and costs of legal action taken because of contraventions of hygiene legislation or because of the sale of unfit or unsatisfactory food;
- civil action taken by food poisoning sufferers, or those aggrieved by injury or trauma from foreign bodies in food;
- food losses due to premature spoilage or damage, because of poor stock rotation, incorrect storage temperature or pest infestations;
- low staff morale, higher turnover with attendant costs and inefficiencies from staff unwilling or unable to tolerate poor standards;
- food complaints and costs of internal investigation and decontamination; and
- loss of production.

Bad hygiene - lower profits!

SUPERVISING FOOD SAFETY (LEVEL 3) An introduction to food safety

Food employees may suffer by:
♦ losing their jobs because of closure, loss of business or because they become long-term carriers of food poisoning organisms, especially salmonella; and
♦ losing overtime or bonuses.

The benefits of high standards of hygiene

♦ Satisfied customers, a good reputation which creates greater confidence and increased business.
♦ Brand protection.
♦ Improved standards of food safety and compliance with food safety legislation.
♦ Less food wastage and increased shelf life.
♦ Good working conditions, higher staff morale and lower staff turnover, which promotes increased productivity.
♦ Reduced risk of food poisoning and food complaints.

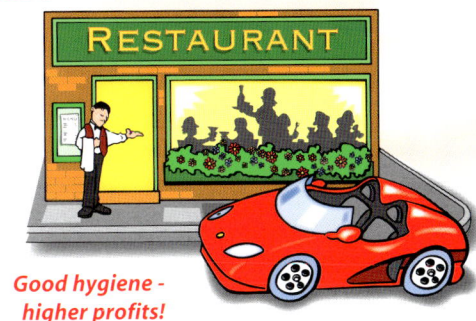

Good hygiene - higher profits!

High-risk foods

High-risk foods are ready-to-eat foods which, under favourable conditions, support the multiplication of pathogenic bacteria and are intended for consumption without treatment which would destroy such organisms. High-risk foods are most likely to be involved in cases of food poisoning. They are usually high in protein and moisture, requiring strict temperature control and protection from contamination and include:
♦ all cooked meat and poultry;
♦ cooked meat products including liquid gravy, stock, pâté and meat pies;
♦ milk, cream, artificial cream, custards and dairy produce;
♦ cooked eggs/products, especially those products made with raw eggs and not thoroughly cooked, for example, mousse, mayonnaise and home-made ice cream;
♦ shellfish and other seafoods, for example, cooked prawns and oysters; and
♦ cooked rice (not high in protein).

Low-risk foods

These foods are rarely implicated in food poisoning and may be stored, suitably packaged, at ambient temperatures. They do not support the multiplication of food poisoning bacteria. Examples include:
♦ preserved food such as jam;
♦ dried foods or food with little available moisture, such as flour, rice, bread, biscuits. On adding liquid to powdered food, such as milk, the food becomes high-risk;
♦ acid foods, such as vinegar or products stored in vinegar;
♦ fermented products, such as salami;
♦ foods with high fat/sugar content, such as chocolate (chocolate is occasionally

responsible for salmonella outbreaks); and
- canned foods, whilst unopened.

Ready-to-eat raw foods

Unfortunately an increasing number of outbreaks of foodborne illness are attributed to the consumption of raw, ready-to-eat foods which are stored at ambient temperatures, for example, salad vegetables, melons, raspberries and unpasteurized apple juice. As these foods don't usually support the multiplication of pathogens, the organisms involved are capable of causing illness in very low numbers, for example, viruses, *E. coli* O157, shigella and parasites.

Salmonella outbreaks have been associated with cut melon, lettuce and apple juice. Lettuce, raspberries and apple juice have been the food vehicle for outbreaks of viral illness and *E. coli* O157. Sewage contamination or bad hygiene practices during harvesting are the most likely causes of outbreaks. Ready-to-eat raw foods should be washed and preferably disinfected before use.

Raw foods (intended for cooking/processing)

Raw foods are often contaminated with large numbers of food poisoning bacteria, for example, raw meat, milk, poultry, eggs and root vegetables contaminated with soil. If raw foods are perishable, they should be stored in a refrigerator separate from high-risk and ready-to-eat food. Raw food may present a serious risk of food poisoning if not heat-treated or cooked thoroughly, especially poultry, products made with raw egg, bivalves, such as oysters, and raw milk.

Food poisoning

Food poisoning is usually an acute illness resulting from eating contaminated or poisonous food. It excludes allergies to food or toxins. The symptoms normally include one or more of the following: abdominal pain, diarrhoea, vomiting and nausea.

Gastroenteritis

This term is used to refer to an inflammation of the stomach and intestinal tract that normally results in diarrhoea.

Carriers

Carriers are people who show no symptoms of illness but excrete food poisoning or foodborne pathogens which may contaminate food, for example, salmonellae or shigellae. Organisms may be excreted intermittently.

Convalescent carriers are people who have recovered from an illness but still harbour the organism. The convalescent state may be quite prolonged and salmonellae are sometimes excreted for several months.

Healthy carriers are people who have displayed no symptoms but harbour and excrete the causative organism. They are unlikely to be suspected of causing illness. Healthy carriers may have become infected with pathogenic bacteria from contact with raw food with which they work, particularly poultry or meat.

SUPERVISING FOOD SAFETY (LEVEL 3) An introduction to food safety

Risk groups

Some groups of people have a much greater risk of getting a foodborne illness. Furthermore, the illness is likely to be more serious and death is more frequent. Risk groups include babies and very young children, the elderly, people already ill, pregnant women and those who are immunocompromised, for example, transplant patients and drug abusers.

THE INCIDENCE OF FOOD POISONING IN ENGLAND & WALES AND SCOTLAND

The annual incidence of food poisoning is unknown. Several million people in England and Wales suffer from gastroenteritis each year; many of these will have food poisoning and a few will die. Those most at risk include the young, the elderly, the immunocompromised and pregnant women.

Salmonella levels have reduced as a result of vaccination of egg-laying poultry and the use of pasteurized liquid egg. The increased amount of training and the implementation of food safety management systems such as HACCP, may also have had an effect.

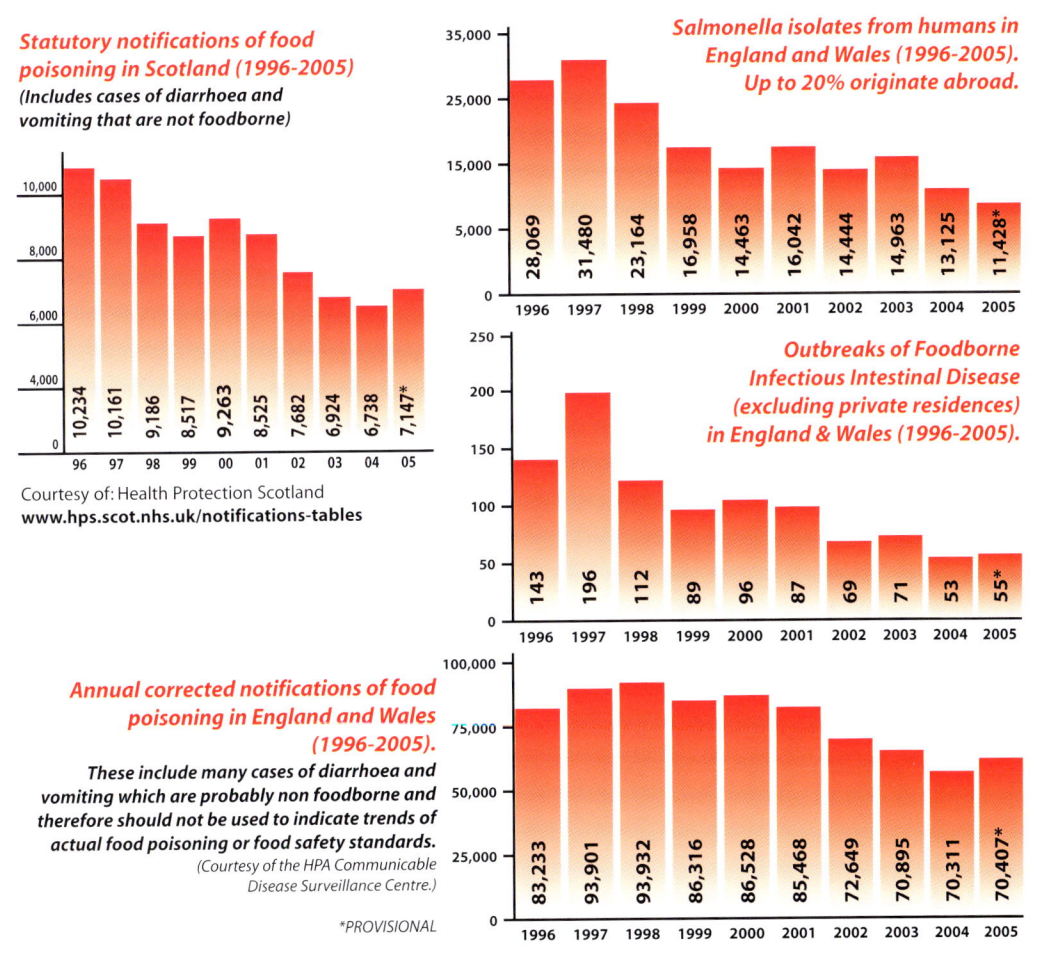

Statutory notifications of food poisoning in Scotland (1996-2005)
(Includes cases of diarrhoea and vomiting that are not foodborne)

Year	96	97	98	99	00	01	02	03	04	05
Cases	10,234	10,161	9,186	8,517	9,263	8,525	7,682	6,924	6,738	7,147*

Courtesy of: Health Protection Scotland
www.hps.scot.nhs.uk/notifications-tables

Salmonella isolates from humans in England and Wales (1996-2005). Up to 20% originate abroad.

Year	1996	1997	1998	1999	2000	2001	2002	2003	2004	2005
Cases	28,069	31,480	23,164	16,958	14,463	16,042	14,444	14,963	13,125	11,428*

Outbreaks of Foodborne Infectious Intestinal Disease (excluding private residences) in England & Wales (1996-2005).

Year	1996	1997	1998	1999	2000	2001	2002	2003	2004	2005
Outbreaks	143	196	112	89	96	87	69	71	53	55*

Annual corrected notifications of food poisoning in England and Wales (1996-2005).
These include many cases of diarrhoea and vomiting which are probably non foodborne and therefore should not be used to indicate trends of actual food poisoning or food safety standards.
(Courtesy of the HPA Communicable Disease Surveillance Centre.)

*PROVISIONAL

Year	1996	1997	1998	1999	2000	2001	2002	2003	2004	2005
Cases	83,233	93,901	93,932	86,316	86,528	85,468	72,649	70,895	70,311	70,407*

2 *Microbiology*

Microbiology is the study of microscopic plants and animals and this includes bacteria, moulds and yeasts. The most important micro-organisms of interest to the food industry are bacteria, and bacteriology is the study of bacteria. If food handlers are to understand food safety and how to prevent food poisoning, they must have some understanding of basic bacteriology.

Bacteria are single-celled micro-organisms which are found everywhere: on raw food and people, in soil, air and water. A micro-organism is an organism that is so small it can only be seen under a powerful microscope. Most bacteria are harmless and some are essential, for example, for breaking down decaying matter. Others are of benefit to the food industry, for example, in the manufacture of cheese and yoghurt. Unfortunately a small number of bacteria cause food spoilage and others, known as pathogens, cause illness including food poisoning.

Commensals are bacteria which live on or in the body without causing illness. Most bacteria on the body are commensals and are part of the normal flora. For example, some species of staphylococcus are found on the skin and in the mouth or nose. Other species are transient and may cause skin infections, such as boils. If harmful species of staphylococcus are transferred to high-risk food, they may cause illness.

The size, shape and structure of bacteria

Bacteria can only be observed under a microscope with a magnification of around 1000 times. Bacteria vary in size from around .001mm to .003mm. Although an individual bacterium cannot be seen, large numbers can be seen as small white or yellow spots on growth media in laboratories. These spots are known as colonies. Large numbers of spoilage organisms may also cause visible effects on food, for example, discolouration, slime and odour.

Bacteria vary considerably in shape:
- Cocci are spherical;
- Spirochaetes are spiral; and
- Rods are sausage-shaped;
- Vibrios are comma-shaped;

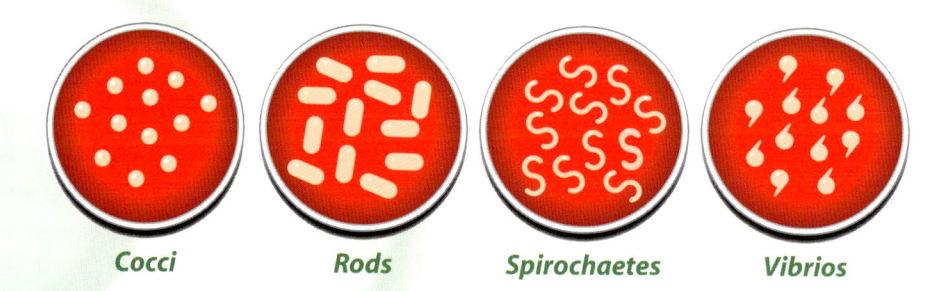

Cocci   *Rods*   *Spirochaetes*   *Vibrios*

Cell wall – a rigid structure that gives the bacterium its shape.
Cell membrane – controls passage of waste and nutrients into and out of the cell.
Cytoplasm – the 'body' of the bacterium.
Nuclear material – the 'brain' of the bacterium (gives genetic characteristics).
Flagella – attachments that allow bacteria to move in liquids.

Although some bacteria can use flagella to swim around in liquids, most bacteria rely on other objects to move them about, for example, moving from one food to another using a table top, a piece of equipment such as a knife or the hands of the food handler. Things which transfer bacteria from one place to another are known as vehicles.

As food poisoning bacteria are commonly found on raw food and people, it is impracticable to operate a food business without food poisoning bacteria being present at one time or another. It is therefore essential to deny them the conditions which would allow them to multiply to a level where they present a risk to customers. (Large numbers of bacteria usually need to be present in food to cause food poisoning.)

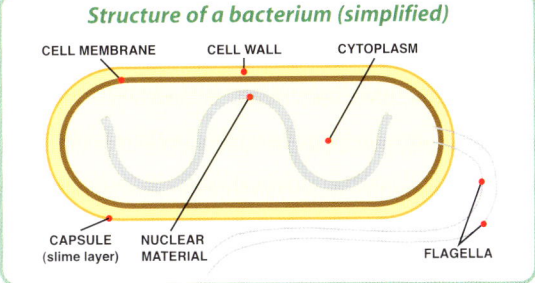

Structure of a bacterium (simplified)

Labels: CELL MEMBRANE, CELL WALL, CYTOPLASM, CAPSULE (slime layer), NUCLEAR MATERIAL, FLAGELLA

Bacterial multiplication

Bacteria reproduce by splitting into two. This process is known as binary fission and the time taken between each division (generation time) varies considerably depending on, among other things, temperature and the nutrients (food) available. In optimum (ideal) conditions some food poisoning bacteria can split in two every ten minutes, although at temperatures of around 10°C it may take up to ten hours or they may stop multiplying. The average generation time of the common food poisoning bacteria under optimum conditions is usually considered to be around 20 minutes. When bacteria are growing and multiplying this is described as the vegetative state.

If food is contaminated a common level of contamination may be around 1000 bacteria per gram of food. If this food provides optimum conditions then within one hour 40 minutes, these bacteria could double every ten minutes and become 1,000,000. This number of bacteria is likely to cause food poisoning. The multiplication of pathogens in food is a hazard.

Nutrients

Food poisoning bacteria obtain their essential basic nutrients from amino acids, fats, vitamins and minerals, which are usually provided by high protein food such as meat, fish and dairy produce. Foods with high sugar and salt content are usually unsuitable and therefore are unlikely to support bacterial multiplication.

Moisture

Bacteria require water to transport nutrients into the cell and take away waste products. The a$_W$ (water activity) of food is the measure of the available water. With the exception of dehydrated products such as milk powder, most foods contain sufficient moisture to enable bacteria to multiply. However, some bacteria can survive dehydration and when liquid is added to the dried food it once again becomes a high-risk food and must be stored under refrigeration.

Acidity and alkalinity (pH)

The pH of a food is measured on a scale of 1 to 14 (hydrogen ion concentration). Acid foods have pH values below 7, alkaline foods above 7 and a pH value of 7 is neutral. Most bacteria will not multiply in a pH below 4.0, i.e. an acid food such as fruit juice. However, if a large number of food poisoning bacteria are introduced into an acid food it may take some time for the bacteria to die. For this reason we must protect acid food from contamination at all times.

Temperature

Bacteria have a maximum and minimum temperature for multiplication as well as an optimum temperature when multiplication is the most rapid. Most food poisoning bacteria grow best at around 37°C (body temperature) although *Clostridium perfringens* prefers 46°C. The common food poisoning bacteria will not multiply below 5°C or above 52°C. However, many can survive outside this temperature range and start multiplying again when temperatures are suitable. The range of temperature, which is likely to encourage the fastest multiplication, is between 20°C and 50°C. Some pathogens will grow between 0°C and 20°C but they multiply more slowly at the lower temperatures. The lowest recorded temperature for the growth of pathogenic bacteria is −2ºC and although pathogens can survive freezing they do not multiply.

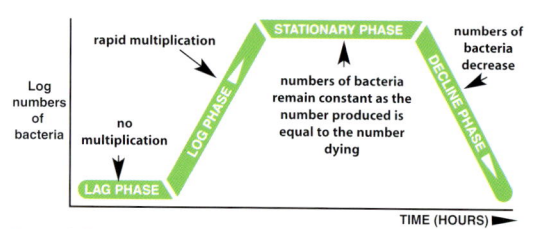

Bacterial growth curve which shows the four stages of bacterial growth when, for example, food is removed from a refrigerator.

Some food spoilage bacteria multiply slowly under refrigeration, which is one of the reasons for food becoming unfit if stored longer than the recommended shelf life.

Psychrophiles are bacteria which prefer temperatures below 20°C. **Mesophiles** prefer temperatures of 20°C to 50°C and this group includes the common food poisoning bacteria. **Thermophiles** multiply most rapidly above 45°C. Large numbers of bacteria may survive freezing and start multiplying when food thaws.

Presence of oxygen

Some bacteria can only multiply in the presence of oxygen and others can only multiply when there is no oxygen. The former bacteria are known as aerobes and the latter anaerobes. Many bacteria can multiply with or without the presence of oxygen and these are called facultative anaerobes, for example, salmonella.

Oxygen is normally present in food except in the case of liquids which have been thoroughly boiled. Cooking, for example, joints of meat, also drives off oxygen and the centre then provides ideal conditions for anaerobes.

Toxin production

Food poisoning bacteria produce toxins (poisons) which cannot be detected by visual inspection. Toxins may be either exotoxins or endotoxins.

Exotoxins are produced during multiplication or sporulation of bacteria. Quite often exotoxins are released into the food and many are heat resistant, so that even if cooking destroys the bacteria, the toxin may remain and cause illness if the food is eaten. This results in a short onset time. Toxins will usually not be produced if food is kept below 5°C or above 63°C and the time at ambient temperature is kept short. Enterotoxins are exotoxins that affect the gastrointestinal tract.

Endotoxins form part of the bacterial cell wall and are released on the death of the bacteria, usually in the intestines of persons consuming contaminated food. If the toxin is produced in the intestine, the onset period, for the first symptoms to appear, will usually be longer than if the toxin is in the food.

Spore formation

Some food poisoning bacteria, such as *Clostridium perfringens*, *Bacillus cereus* and *Clostridium botulinum* are able to form spores which are capable of surviving unfavourable conditions such as high temperatures, dehydration and the use of disinfectants. Spores are round protective bodies which form inside the bacterial cell and may allow survival for many years without food and water. They cannot be detected by visual inspection. Spores survive normal cooking and germinate during long, slow cooling. The vegetative bacteria released will then start multiplying and may produce toxins.

Temperatures in excess of 100°C are often required for long periods (as much as five hours) to destroy spores. The temperature used to ensure the safety of low-acid canned food, by destroying spores of *Clostridium botulinum*, is the equivalent of 121°C for three minutes.

Competition

When there are many different bacteria present, they will compete for the same food. Fortunately, most food poisoning bacteria are not as competitive as the normal flora found on food and, unless present in high numbers, will usually die.

Destruction of bacteria

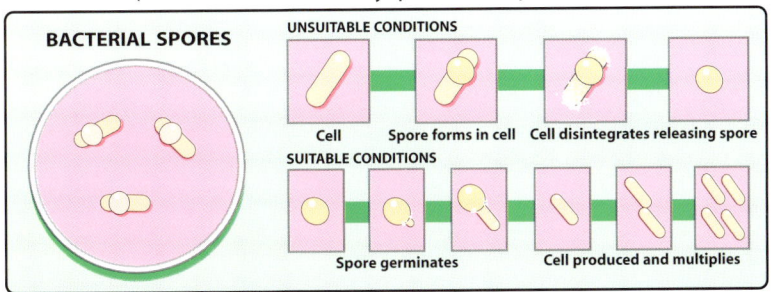

Food poisoning bacteria can be destroyed by using high temperatures for sufficient time. The higher the temperature, the shorter the time required. However, the type of bacteria (whether or not they produce spores), the number of bacteria present and the type of food also affect the time needed to kill bacteria and make the food safe. Bacteria will start to die at around 55°C. However, a core temperature of greater than 75°C is required when cooking food to be reasonably confident that most harmful bacteria will have been destroyed.

Unfortunately, much higher temperatures are required to destroy toxins and spores produced by some food poisoning bacteria. Spores are much more resistant to drying, boiling, disinfectants and other conditions, which usually destroy vegetative food poisoning bacteria. The survival of bacteria, spores or toxins is a hazard.

Bacteria can also be destroyed by irradiation, chemicals such as nitrates, salt or sugar, u/v light, steam or the use of disinfectants such as bleach. Freezing cannot be used to destroy bacteria as most will survive the freezing process and long periods of storage at freezing temperatures.

Moulds

Moulds are aerobic chlorophyll-free fungi which produce thread-like filaments (hyphae) and form a branched network of mycelium. Moulds, which may be black, white or of various colours, will grow on most foods, whether moist or dry, acid or alkaline and high in salt or sugar concentrations. The optimum growth temperature is usually 20°C to 30°C, although they will grow well over a wide range of temperatures and may cause problems in refrigerators. Growth has been recorded as low as -10°C. High humidities and fluctuating temperatures accelerate mould growth.

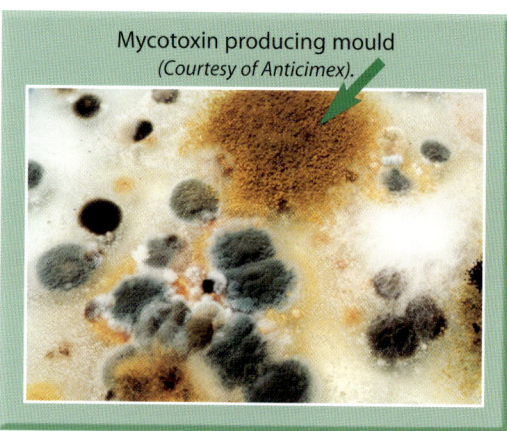

Mycotoxin producing mould (Courtesy of Anticimex).

Moulds commonly affect bread and other bakery products, and although spores are usually destroyed in baking, subsequent contamination is difficult to avoid. Mould inhibitors are usually added to bread.

Food must always be stored in accordance with the manufacturer's instructions and never sold outside its 'use-by' date. Mishandling of vacuum packs of cheese may result in punctures and consequential mould growth. As the mycelium grows over the food, hyphae penetrate the substance and consequently mould soon returns if scraped off the surface. Regular checking of stock is imperative to avoid customer complaints. The presence of mould on food is usually considered to render it unfit for human consumption. Cheeses produced with specific moulds are an exception.

Yeasts

Yeasts are microscopic fungi which reproduce by budding. Most yeasts grow best in the presence of oxygen, although fermentative types may grow slowly anaerobically. The majority of yeasts prefer acid foods (pH 4 to 4.5) with a reasonable level of available moisture. However, many yeasts will grow in high concentrations of sugar and salt. The optimum growth temperature for yeast is around 25°C to 30°C with a maximum of around 47°C. Some yeasts can grow slowly at 0°C and below.

Yeasts are used in the manufacture of foods such as bread, beer and vinegar. However, they cause spoilage of many foods including jam, fruit juice, honey, meats and wines.

Viruses

Viruses are even smaller than bacteria and can only be seen under a very powerful electron microscope. They multiply in living cells, not in food. Some viruses cause illness, including viral gastroenteritis and hepatitis A.

Protozoa

Protozoa are single-celled organisms which form the basis of the food chain. They live in most habitats such as oceans, soil and decaying matter. Some are pathogenic and usually result in waterborne outbreaks. They do not multiply in food but their cysts may remain infectious in foods for a long time. Furthermore, they have a low infective dose, i.e. only small numbers of cysts are required to cause illness. Two pathogenic protozoa causing illness in the UK are *Cryptosporidium parvum* and *Giardia lamblia*.

Key points

- Bacteria are found everywhere but can only be seen under a microscope.
- Food businesses cannot operate without food poisoning bacteria being present at one time or another.
- Bacteria rely on food, people and equipment to move about in food premises.
- Bacteria require food, moisture, warmth and time to multiply.
- The common food poisoning bacteria prefer a temperature range of 20°C to 50°C for rapid multiplication.
- In optimum conditions, some food poisoning bacteria can multiply every ten minutes. The multiplication of pathogens within food is a hazard.
- Temperatures above 75°C are used to destroy bacteria but some exotoxins and spores may survive boiling for a considerable period. Survival of bacteria, spores or toxins is a hazard.
- Spores or toxins in food cannot be detected by visual inspection.
- Most food poisoning bacteria will not multiply in refrigerators below 5°C, but they will survive freezing.
- Food poisoning bacteria do not multiply in high acid food, high salt or sugar concentrations or dried foods (until reconstituted).

SUPERVISING FOOD SAFETY (LEVEL 3) Food contamination and its prevention

3 Food contamination and its prevention

Contamination of food is a major hazard* and may be considered as the occurrence of any objectionable matter in or on the food. Therefore, carcasses may be contaminated with faecal material, high-risk food may be contaminated with spoilage or food poisoning bacteria and flour may be contaminated with rodent hairs. To prevent the consumption of food which is unacceptable or unsafe, contamination must be kept to a minimum.

There are four types of contamination/hazards:

- *Microbiological hazards caused by bacteria, moulds, viruses (micro-organisms) or parasites.* Usually occurs in food premises because of ignorance, inadequate space, poor design or because of food handlers taking short cuts. In the early stages it will not be detectable. Contamination of this sort is the most serious and may result in food spoilage, food poisoning or even death.
- *Physical hazards from foreign bodies including insects.* Physical contamination may render food unfit or unsafe but often involves pieces of paper, plastic, metal or string and is usually unpleasant or a nuisance.
- *Chemical hazards.* Examples include pesticides on fruit and residues from cleaning chemicals.
- *Allergenic hazards.* Examples include peanuts, milk, eggs and cereals.

MICROBIOLOGICAL HAZARDS

Bacterial contamination is the most significant as it results in large amounts of spoilt food and unacceptable numbers of food poisoning cases. Food poisoning bacteria may be brought into food premises by the following sources:

- food handlers/visitors;
- raw foods including poultry, meat, eggs, milk, fish and shellfish and water especially when polluted with sewage or animal faeces. Vegetables or fruit may become contaminated from manure or polluted irrigation water;
- insects, rodents, animals and birds; and
- from the environment, including soil and dust.

Mould spores will be present in the atmosphere, on surfaces, especially damp surfaces, and on mouldy food. Food should always be covered and mouldy food must be segregated. Furthermore, mould must not be allowed to grow on walls, ceilings and window frames. Mould growth often occurs if food is stored at the wrong temperature, at high humidity and in excess of the recommended shelf life. It may also

* A food safety hazard is anything with the potential to cause harm to the consumer.

SUPERVISING FOOD SAFETY (LEVEL 3) Food contamination and its prevention

affect cheese stored in vacuum packs which are pierced. Canned foods which are removed from cases opened with unguarded craft knives may become punctured, thus giving rise to mould growth inside the can.

Viruses are usually brought into food premises by food handlers who are carriers, or on raw food such as shellfish which have been grown in sewage-polluted water.

Vehicles and routes of bacterial contamination

Sometimes bacteria pass directly from the source to high-risk food, but as bacteria are largely static and as the sources are not always in direct contact with food, the bacteria have to rely on other things to transfer them to food. These things are known as vehicles of contamination and the main ones are:

- hands;
- hand-contact surfaces; and
- cloths and equipment;
- food-contact surfaces.

Cross-contamination can be defined as 'the transfer of bacteria from contaminated foods (usually raw) to other foods'. This includes direct contact, drip and indirect contamination by, for example, hands not washed between raw and cooked food preparation, or using the same equipment or work surfaces for raw and high-risk food. The path along which bacteria are transferred from the source to the food is known as the route. Knowledge of sources, vehicles and routes is vital to food poisoning prevention, as different controls apply to each. It must be assumed that all sources are contaminated, i.e. every worker is a carrier and all raw meat, milk, animals, insects, used equipment and the surrounding environment are contaminated.

SOURCES, VEHICLES AND ROUTES OF CONTAMINATION

Prevention of contamination depends on either removing the sources, or putting barriers between them and the vehicles or between them and food. Thus human access to food must be restricted, raw foods handled in separate areas, vermin excluded and work areas enclosed in suitably constructed and ventilated rooms.

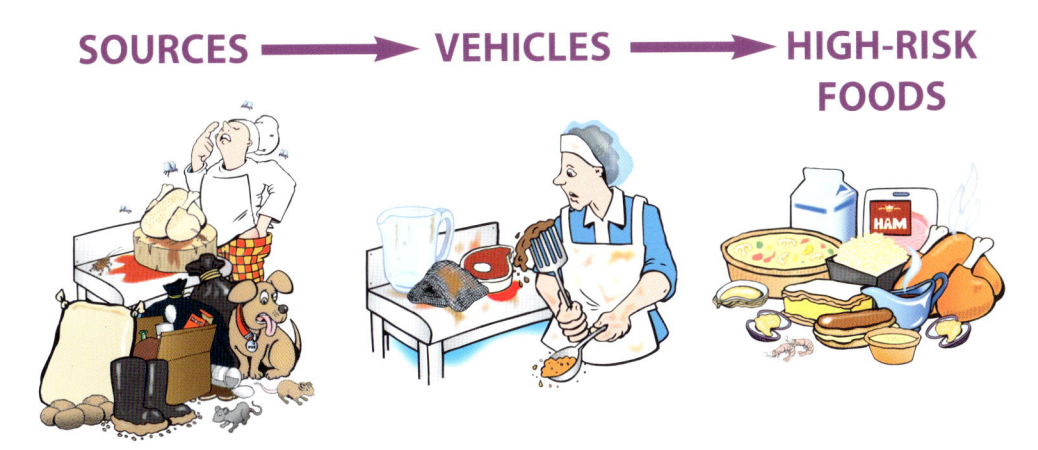

SOURCES ⟶ VEHICLES ⟶ HIGH-RISK FOODS

SUPERVISING FOOD SAFETY (LEVEL 3) Food contamination and its prevention

Similarly, vehicles must, where possible, be excluded. Handling should be minimized, wiping cloths used sparingly or destroyed after each use, hand-contact surfaces, such as tap handles, replaced with knee or electronically operated taps, and the number of surfaces with which the food comes into contact limited.

In the nature of food preparation, however, routes between sources and vehicles survive, giving rise to contaminated vehicles. Consequently, routes must be disrupted by cleaning and disinfection. For example, should a work surface come into contact with a contaminated source, raw meat for instance, the surface must be cleaned and disinfected before it is used for cooked meat.

CHECK LIST FOR CONTAMINATION CONTROL

- Purchase food and raw materials from known, reliable and hygienic suppliers.
- Accept deliveries only if transported in clean, properly equipped vehicles, with clean drivers wearing satisfactory protective clothing. Refrigerated vehicles may be necessary.
- Inspect deliveries immediately on arrival. Reject or segregate any damaged, unfit or contaminated material. Where relevant, check temperature, codes and date markings and reject out-of-date food.
- After checking, remove deliveries immediately to appropriate storage, refrigerator or cold store.

Unsatisfactory deliveries must be rejected

- Keep any unfit food, chemicals and refuse away from stored food. Use only food containers for storing food.
- Keep high-risk foods apart from raw foods at all times, in separate areas with separate utensils and equipment. Colour coding is useful. Separate food handlers are recommended.
- Maintain scrupulous personal hygiene at all times and handle food as little as possible. Exclude potential carriers.
- Keep food covered or otherwise protected unless it is actually being processed or prepared, in which case bring food out only when needed. Do not leave food lying around.
- Keep premises, equipment and utensils clean and in good condition and repair. Report or remedy defects with the minimum of delay. Disinfect food-contact surfaces, hand-contact surfaces and cleaning equipment.
- Ensure that all empty containers are clean and disinfected prior to filling with food.
- Control cleaning materials, particularly wiping cloths. Keep cleaning materials

away from food. Remove food and food containers before cleaning. Care must be taken to ensure that all cleaning residues, including water, are drained from food equipment and pipes. Always clean from high-risk areas to low-risk areas.

- Remove waste food and refuse from food areas as soon as practicable. Store in appropriate containers, away from food.
- Maintain an active pest control programme.
- Control visitors and maintenance workers in high-risk areas. Ensure hygiene disciplines apply to all personnel, including management.
- Inspect food areas and processes frequently, act on any defects or unhygienic practices. Train staff and monitor performance. Food handlers and engineers must be aware of the bacteriological and physical contamination they may introduce.
- Ensure adequate thawing of foods, separate from other foods.
- Make suitable provisions for cooling food prior to refrigeration.

PHYSICAL HAZARDS

Foreign bodies found in food may be brought into food premises with the raw materials or introduced during storage, preparation, service or display. It is essential that supervisors are aware of the types of foreign bodies commonly found in their particular sector of the food industry and that they take all reasonable precautions and exercise all due diligence to secure their removal or prevent their introduction. Product traceability systems must be introduced. A record should be kept of all customer complaints and steps should be taken to identify the source of the contaminant.

Contamination of food by extraneous matter will cause customer dissatisfaction and may result in bad publicity. If media coverage results, the impact on the business can be disastrous leading, in the worst possible case, to loss of product confidence and even company viability. It is therefore in the interests of the business to minimize the risk of foreign body contamination.

Intrinsic foreign bodies, such as bones in chicken meat or stalks in vegetables, should be minimized by care in harvesting and processing, although foreign body detection and removal systems, such as the use of inspection belts, will also be necessary. The presence of foreign bodies in food, such as glass or rodent droppings, is usually of greater concern as this indicates a breakdown in hygiene and will not be tolerated by the consumer.

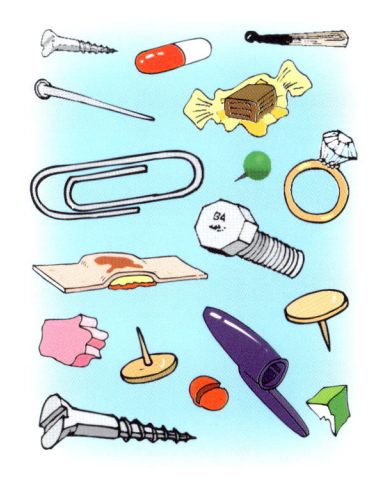

Common foreign bodies found in food

SUPERVISING FOOD SAFETY (LEVEL 3) Food contamination and its prevention

Although in the minority, some foreign bodies may be considered a serious health hazard, such as glass, stones, wire or rodent droppings, which may result in cut mouths, dental damage, choking or illness.

However, all foreign bodies are, at the very least, a nuisance and food businesses must implement appropriate systems to prevent or remove such contamination. Their presence in food is likely to be an offence under food safety legislation. The hazard analysis and critical control point system (HACCP) provides the most effective preventive approach, and will be extremely useful if the company wishes to avail itself of the due-diligence defence in the event of a prosecution.

IDENTIFYING PHYSICAL HAZARDS AND CONTROL MEASURES
Raw materials

The variable nature of raw material quality may be a significant problem in food processing. Raw materials can be a major source of extraneous matter and food manufacturers use a range of cleaning, sorting and grading operations to separate out the offending material. In the manufacture of frozen peas for example, stones, metal screws, cigarette ends, stalks, sticks, caterpillars and dirt often accompany the vined peas as they arrive at the factory.

Control measures should include specifications to detail maximum permissible levels of contaminants in the incoming raw materials. By agreeing specifications with all suppliers and monitoring and evaluating the supplier performance in meeting the specifications, the company has an effective tool in minimizing the risk posed by extraneous matter.

Before using raw materials, cleaning or washing and inspection may need to be carried out. Most physical contamination has to be removed by food handlers as the vegetables pass along an illuminated inspection belt.

Liquids used in food production should be filtered and powders sieved. Filters, screens and sieves should be as fine as possible and must be cleaned and checked regularly. Worn equipment must be replaced. Wooden-framed sieves are usually unacceptable.

Packaging materials

Packaging may be a source of extraneous matter in the form of warehouse and transport dirt/dust, wood from the pallets, paper and polythene strips from over-wraps and a variety of insects and even rodents. Containers (cans, jars, bottles and plastic pots) may be used directly for filling with minimal cleaning and any rogue material in the container (metal splinters, glass, dirt, insects, etc.) may end up in the final product.

Staples, cardboard, string, fibres, cloth, rubber, plastic and polythene

Food may be delivered in various containers including paper sacks, cardboard boxes and polythene bags. Particular care is necessary when emptying containers to avoid contamination of food. As far as practicable, all unpacking and packing should be carried out in areas separate from food production or preparation, if open food is exposed to risk of contamination.

String removed from hessian sacks and ties removed from bags should immediately be placed in suitable containers provided specifically for the purpose. As an extra precaution, coloured string may be specified to aid detection should it end up in the product. Paper sacks should be cut open, although care must be exercised to ensure pieces of paper do not finish up in the food. It is preferable for raw materials to be emptied into suitable lidded containers and not dispensed direct from paper sacks.

Particular care is needed to ensure that staples, which tend to fly considerable distances when boxes are prised open, do not contaminate food. Suppliers should be requested to use adhesive tape to fasten boxes, instead of staples. Many products are delivered in black polythene bags and small pieces of polythene often end up in the product.

Effective measures in terms of good hygiene practice should be adopted within the HACCP scheme to minimize the risk of contamination. An example would be the use of secondary packaging which is removed prior to primary packaging material entering a high-risk area.

The building, installations and equipment
Wood splinters

As far as possible the use of wood, especially soft wood, should be eliminated from food production areas. Wooden containers used for transporting raw materials should be phased out. Pallets should not be double stacked over open food.

Bolts, nuts and other pieces of metal

As far as practicable nuts should be self-locking. Bolts, nuts and screws should be non-corroding and positioned to ensure that, should they fall off equipment, they do not drop into the food.

Hazards from wood splinters, rust and flaking paint

Flaking paint or rust

Ceiling structure, pipes or equipment should be non-flaking and rust-free. This is especially important when such fixtures are positioned directly above open products. In some older factories this problem is very difficult to overcome and consequently additional protection is necessary, for example, enclosed systems for conveying food and empty containers such as cans. New food premises should be designed so that fixtures, ducts and pipes are not suspended over working areas or food if the product is exposed to risk of contamination, for example, from condensation.

Grease and oil

Wherever necessary, food-grade grease and lubricants should be used. It is important that engineers use the minimum amount necessary to lubricate moving parts and that grease is not left on the machine. Careful control will ensure the absence of complaints relating to grease in food. It is preferable for motors not to be positioned above open food. When this occurs, suitable non-corroding, cleansable drip-trays should be fixed underneath to catch oil spillages.

Glass

As far as practicable the use of ordinary glass should be minimized in food rooms. Perspex or wired glass windows should be used. Protective sleeves or diffusers should be fitted to fluorescent tubes in any rooms where breakage would expose food to risk of contamination. Dials and gauges on equipment should be unbreakable. Mirrors and glass thermometers should not be used. Unauthorized glass containers or equipment should not be brought into food rooms. All food businesses should have a glass policy especially to deal with glass breakages. When replacing or cleaning fluorescent tubes or diffusers, food and containers should be removed or protected so there is no risk of contamination.

In the event of breakage, food preparation should stop. All potentially contaminated food should be discarded. Food containers should be checked for broken glass and cleaned. All broken glass should be be swept up and disposed of in a safe manner. The brush used should be discarded as it is likely to contain broken glass. The area

Hazards from broken glass dials and windows

should be fully cleaned and inspected before food preparation starts again. Staff will require appropriate instruction and/or training to ensure they respond correctly to breakages.

In factories, optical scanners, filters, sieves, x-ray machines and air separation systems may be used to detect and/or remove glass from food. In the event of products being contaminated with glass it may be necessary to recall the food and notify the environmental health department. Breakages when filling glass jars or bottles are always likely and particular care is needed to ensure containers adjacent to fillers when a breakage occurs are discarded. Furthermore, a suitable system, e.g. inverting and washing or blasting with air, is necessary to minimize the risk of broken glass being present in a container just prior to filling.

Notices

Notices used for warnings, advice or instructions should be properly fixed and permanent. Sheets of paper sellotaped to equipment or close to open food are unacceptable. Recipe instructions should be enclosed in sealed polythene bags. Notice boards should be kept out of areas where open food is handled and should be covered in perspex or similar sheeting.

SUPERVISING FOOD SAFETY (LEVEL 3) Food contamination and its prevention

Food handlers

Contaminants, which originate from personnel, include earrings, hair, fingernails, buttons, combs and pen tops. Protective clothing, including head covering, must be of a suitable type and worn correctly. The personal hygiene of food handlers must be beyond reproach, and earrings and jewellery, other than wedding rings, should not be worn. Pencils, pens and pieces of chalk must not be used in situations which expose food to risk of contamination, for example, near filling hoppers and mixing vessels.

Sweet papers, cigarette ends and matches are common contaminants and staff should not eat sweets, chew gum or smoke in food rooms. Regular training and reinforcement, such as posters, should be used together with strict supervision and enforcement of company rules.

Cleaning activities

Care must be taken during cleaning and all staff involved should be trained to ensure they do not expose products to risk of contamination by using worn equipment, especially brushes which are likely to lose their bristles, or by using inappropriate methods such as high pressure spraying during the production of open food. Particular care must be exercised when using paper towels or cloths to ensure small pieces of paper or cloth do not end up in the product.

Maintenance operatives/tradesmen

Engineers must be trained/briefed to take extra care when working with food equipment to ensure that they do not leave loose nuts, swarf and pieces of wire in food rooms on completion of maintenance. Written instructions may be useful. Temporary repairs with string should be avoided. It is good practice for managers to check areas where engineers or contractors have been working before food handling commences.

During production, areas which are being decorated or where repair or maintenance work is being carried out must be suitably segregated by screens, such as heavy-duty polythene, to avoid exposing product to risk of contamination. Workers should be closely supervised during maintenance activities. Maintenance workers should not wear soiled overalls and suitable protective clothing may be provided by the food business. They should not stand on or climb over machinery or open food if there is the slightest risk of introducing contamination. They should not smoke or eat sweets and should observe good hygiene practices. If necessary, all food and food containers should be removed or protected with clean polythene sheeting. The use of ladders over open food or hoppers can result in dirt falling off shoes or rungs and ending up in the final product. After the work has been completed all tools, screws, swarf, grease, etc. must be removed and the area cleaned and, if necessary, disinfected before use. Whenever possible, equipment should be removed from food areas for repair.

SUPERVISING FOOD SAFETY (LEVEL 3) Food contamination and its prevention

Pests and pest control

Rodents, rodent hairs and droppings may be brought into food premises with the raw materials or introduced during the preparation or storage of food in infested premises. Food showing evidence of rodent contamination is unfit and should be rejected.

Insects, larvae and eggs may also be present in raw materials, although some may find their way into food rooms via openings. Several types of insect multiply rapidly and infestations can soon spread throughout food premises. Infested food should be discarded and appropriate control measures introduced. A reputable pest control contractor, experienced at working with food businesses, should be employed to lay rodent bait or traps and control pest infestations should they arise.

Bad pest control is likely to result in food contamination. For example, electronic fly killers positioned above open food, work surfaces or containers will probably result in dead insects in the food, as will the use of insecticides to destroy flying insects, for example, sprays, in the presence of open food.

Cleaners and other staff must be instructed not to touch bait boxes, unless authorized to do so, and never to put bait boxes on shelves above open products whilst cleaning is being undertaken.

Electronic fly killer exposing clean food containers to risk of contamination

Customer contamination

Customers may contaminate food which is not adequately protected, especially when they serve themselves. Handling and sneezing over food is probable and inquisitive customers may break seals to examine the contents of jars and tubs. Furthermore, malicious tampering of products in supermarkets continues to pose a threat to manufacturers and retailers. Finally, contamination of the product may occur in the consumer's home and this should be considered when investigating a complaint.

All reasonable precautions and all due diligence

A food company facing a prosecution as a result of selling a contaminated product will need to demonstrate that they have installed and used an effective, documented detection and rejection system, which is checked regularly, if they are to successfully use the due-diligence defence provided in food safety legislation. It will be up to the courts to decide what is 'reasonable' having regard to good trade practice, industry hygiene guides and the risk and consequences in relation to cost.

Foreign body detection and removal in food manufacturing

No system can guarantee to remove every contaminant and the effectiveness of a particular machine or system will depend on the type of foreign body, the initial level of contamination and the maintenance of the equipment. The performance of most machines will deteriorate with age and use and constant testing is essential. There are many contaminant detection and removal systems available including:

- metal detection systems;
- X-ray systems;
- sieves and filtration;
- optical systems, including colour sorters and scanners;
- magnets;
- air or liquid separation systems; and
- the use of operatives, for example, as spotters, on bottle lines or illuminated inspection belts.

CHEMICAL HAZARDS

Unwanted chemicals can enter foodstuffs during:

- growth, for example, veterinary drugs, fertilizers, pesticides and environmental contaminants such as lead or dioxins;
- processing or food preparation, for example, oil, cleaning chemicals or insecticides;
- transport, as a result of spillage or leakage; and
- sale, for example, cleaning chemicals, insecticides and leaking of such things as plasticizers from packaging. Chemicals may cause acute poisoning or cause long-term illnesses such as cancer.

Cleaning chemicals

To avoid taint, some cleaning chemicals, such as phenols and perfumed soap, must not be used in food premises, especially by those handling dairy/fatty foods. All cleaning materials must be kept in properly labelled containers and stored in a manner which obviates any risk of contamination.

ALLERGENIC HAZARDS

Food allergies are an increasing problem for the food industry including caterers. Food allergens cause the body's immune system to react, often within minutes but sometimes within hours. In serious cases a person may have an anaphylactic

Chemicals must not be stored in food containers or bottles

shock which is life threatening. Even minute amounts of the allergen can result in serious problems. Peanut and other nut allergies are often very severe. The first exposure to a specific allergen does not produce symptoms; however, subsequent exposure results in an allergic response. Symptoms usually include some of the following:

- generalized flushing of the skin;

SUPERVISING FOOD SAFETY (LEVEL 3) Food contamination and its prevention

- nettle rash;
- swelling of the throat and mouth;
- difficulty in swallowing or speaking;
- severe asthma;
- abdominal pain, nausea and/or vomiting;
- sudden feeling of weakness (fall in blood pressure); and
- collapse and unconsciousness.

Food intolerances are usually less severe and do not involve the immune system. They may be due to a lack of enzymes or a response to an irritant.

*Foods which commonly contain allergens include:

- Peanuts – also called groundnuts, are found in many foods, including sauces, cakes and desserts, Indonesian, Thai, Indian, Bangladeshi dishes and peanut flour and groundnut oil.
- Nuts – these include walnuts, hazelnuts, brazil nuts, cashew, pecan, pistachio, macadamia, Queensland nuts and almonds. Found in sauces, desserts, crackers, bread, ice cream, oils, and marzipan.
- Milk – including lactose, in liquid or in powder form, in yoghurt, cream, cheese, butter and other milk products. Ready-made or glazed dishes may contain milk powder.
- Eggs – found in mayonnaise, cakes, mousses, pasta, sauces and quiche. Sometimes used to bind meat in burgers, or to provide a glaze.
- Fish – e.g. anchovies used in salad dressings, sauces, relishes and on pizzas.
- Shellfish – including prawns, scampi, mussels, lobster and crab. Shrimp paste and oyster sauce are found in Chinese and Thai dishes.
- Soya – may be found as tofu, bean curd, soya flour, and textured soya protein. Also found in ice cream, sauces, desserts, meat products and vegetarian products, e.g. veggie burgers.
- Cereals containing gluten – coeliacs need to avoid wheat, rye and barley, oats, spelt and kamut and foods made from these. Bread, pasta, cakes, pastry, and meat products may contain wheat flour. Soups and sauces, dusted, battered or bread crumbed foods may contain flour.
- Sesame seeds – used in bread and breadsticks. Sesame paste (Tahini) in Greek or Turkish dishes, including hummus. Sesame seed oil used in cooking or salad dressings.
- Mustard.
- Celery and celeriac.

Some fruits such as strawberries and kiwi fruit, and lupin flour can cause problems, in addition to colourants, artificial flavourings and preservatives such as sulphur dioxide and sulphites all pose a risk to allergy sufferers.

*Courtesy of the Food Standards Agency (Safer food, better business)

Control of allergenic hazards

Manufacturers must exercise particular care during food production to ensure allergens do not contaminate other products, for example, dust from nuts does not end up contaminating a product that does not normally contain nuts. Cleaning to remove all traces of contamination can be quite difficult and therefore many factories use completely separate production lines or even different factories. Dust can be spread through ventilation systems or involve cross-contamination from cloths, cleaning equipment or personal.

Food businesses should implement an allergen control system based on HACCP and prerequisite programmes to reduce risk from allergens. This will involve using reputable suppliers and branded goods, with all ingredients and foods clearly labelled; satisfactory packaging and segregated storage; using specific equipment for preparation, cooking etc.; segregated displays; separate serving utensils and clear labelling. Ingredient information must be available for all products and staff should know how to check this. In the event of a product becoming contaminated with an allergen it must be discarded or dealt with as a contaminated product.

If there is any risk of a product containing an allergen, it must be clearly labelled. Requirements for labelling allergens are defined in the Food Labelling (Amendment) (England) (No. 2) Regulations 2004. Foods which are identified as most likely to be allergens must always be clearly labelled.

In catering, effective communication and knowledge of all ingredients are essential to reduce the risk from allergens. Don't guess. Clear menu descriptions identifying potential allergenic ingredients should be provided e.g. cooked in ground nut oil. Always update the menu when ingredients or recipes are changed. Staff must be instructed and trained about allergens and the implementation of effective control measures. Regular audits and effective supervision are important to ensure control measures are working.

When a customer confirms they are allergic to a particular food, the person taking the order must provide accurate information to the person preparing the food. It is not just the menu item that may contain the allergen, it could be sauce used to make a garnish, it may be the oil used to cook the food or the allergen may be introduced because of a failure to effectively wash the hands or clean preparation equipment. Allergens won't usually be destroyed by cooking.

All staff should be aware of the action to take in the event of a customer having an anaphylaxis (severe allergic reaction as a result of a susceptible person eating a food containing an allergen).

(The customer may have a pre-loaded adrenaline injection kit which they use as soon as a serious reaction is suspected.)

The customer should not be moved and an ambulance with a paramedic should be called using the emergency number. You should explain that the customer could have anaphylaxis (pronounced 'anna-fill-axis')*.

*For more information on allergens contact: www.anaphylaxis.org.uk

SUPERVISING FOOD SAFETY (LEVEL 3) Food contamination and its prevention

Key points

- Contamination may be defined as the presence or introduction of a hazard and is a major concern.
- There are four types of hazard/contamination: microbiological, foreign bodies, chemicals and allergens.
- Sources of food poisoning bacteria include people, raw foods, pests and the environment.
- Vehicles of contamination include hands, cloths and equipment, hand-contact surfaces and food-contact surfaces.
- Routes are the path bacteria take when being transferred from sources to high-risk food.
- Routes can be disrupted by good design, good practice and cleaning and disinfection.
- Physical contamination results from packaging, the building and equipment, notices, food handlers, cleaning activities, pests and customer contamination
- All reasonable precautions and all due diligence should be taken to avoid prosecution as a result of the sale of contaminated food.
- Chemical contamination can occur during growth, processing/preparation, transport or sale.

4 Food poisoning and foodborne disease

Food poisoning is an acute illness which usually occurs within 1 to 36 hours of eating contaminated or poisonous food. Symptoms normally last from one to seven days and may include diarrhoea, vomiting, abdominal pain, nausea, fever, dehydration and prostration.

Food poisoning may be caused by:
- bacteria or their toxins;
- poisonous fish, including scombrotoxic fish poisoning;
- chemicals such as insecticides, excessive additives and fungicides;
- metals such as lead, copper and mercury;
- poisonous plants such as deadly nightshade, toadstools; and
- moulds (mycotoxins).

Bacteria are responsible for most food poisoning cases, with poisonous fish, plants, chemicals or metals occasionally causing problems. Mycotoxins rarely cause illness in the UK. Viral gastroenteritis is very common but is dealt with as a foodborne disease: Viruses don't multiply in food and only a few viruses are needed to cause illness.

Causative agent (organism)
The causative agent is the bacterium, toxin or poison that contaminates the food and causes food poisoning when the food is consumed.

Onset or incubation period
The onset period is the time between consuming the contaminated food and the first signs of illness.

The food vehicle
The food vehicle is the food consumed that contains the causative agent.

The source
The source is the point from which the causative agent first enters the specific food chain, for example, a cow or a hen. It may also be considered to be the vehicle that brings the causative agent into the food premises responsible for the outbreak, for example, a person, raw milk or an egg.

IMPORTANT FOOD POISONING BACTERIA
Salmonella
Sources
The intestines of ill people and carriers, animals, birds and animal food, raw meat, raw poultry, raw milk, raw eggs, pets, rodents, terrapins, faeces, flies, insects and sewage/water.

SUPERVISING FOOD SAFETY (LEVEL 3) Food poisoning and foodborne disease

Common food vehicles

Undercooked or contaminated cooked meat and poultry, raw milk, raw eggs and uncooked foods using raw eggs in their preparation, for example, mayonnaise, mousses and tiramisu, cut melon, bean sprouts, dried coconut, salad vegetables and chocolate.

Onset period

6 to 72 hours, usually 12 to 36 hours. Endotoxin in intestine (infective food poisoning).

Symptoms and duration of illness

Abdominal pain, diarrhoea, nausea, vomiting, fever and headache. The duration is usually one to seven days. Occasionally deaths are recorded usually involving the elderly, the very young and people who are already ill.

Specific characteristics

Usually requires millions of bacteria to cause illness. However, outbreaks involving low numbers have been recorded in food vehicles with high fat content, such as chocolate, milk and cheese. In such cases the incubation period may be up to 10 days. Salmonella multiplies from 7°C to 47°C under aerobic or anaerobic conditions.

Specific control measures

- Sterilize animal feed and avoid subsequent contamination.
- Segregate ill animals.
- Hygienic transport from farm to abattoir (avoid overcrowding).
- Hygienic slaughtering.
- Prevent cross-contamination between raw and high-risk food from storage through to serving.
- Complete thawing of frozen poultry.
- Thorough cooking to above 75°C. Use heat-treated milk.
- Double-wash raw, ready-to-eat salads and fruit.
- High standards of personal hygiene, especially handwashing after visiting the toilet and before handling high-risk food.
- Exclude symptomatic food handlers.
- Effective cleaning and disinfection.
- Chlorination of water.
- Safe sewage disposal.
- Exclude pests and animals from food premises or food contact.

Clostridium perfringens

Sources

Intestines of humans and animals, faeces and sewage, soil, dust, insects, raw meat and poultry.

Common food vehicles

Rolled joints, casseroles, stews, sauces, mince and meat pies when cooking has removed oxygen.

Onset period
4 to 24 hours, usually 8 to 12 hours. Enterotoxin produced in the intestines. Infective food poisoning.

Symptoms and duration of illness
Abdominal pain and diarrhoea. Vomiting is rare. Symptoms usually last 12 to 48 hours.

Specific characteristics
Clostridium multiplies between 10°C and 52°C under anaerobic conditions. The optimum temperature is between 43°C and 47°C. At 46°C *Clostridium perfringens* can double every ten minutes. It produces spores which can survive high temperatures and dehydration. Illness usually results from consuming millions of organisms. Spores germinate as a result of normal cooking temperatures and long, slow cooling allows the vegetative bacteria to multiply rapidly. Mild reheating may not destroy these bacteria.

Specific control measures
- Separate raw and high-risk foods, especially meat and vegetables.
- Use ready prepared and washed root vegetables to avoid bringing soil into the kitchen. Double wash salad vegetables such as lettuce.
- Strict temperature control.
- Cook or reheat food to at least 75°C and then serve immediately or store above 63°C.
- Maximum joint sizes 2.25 kg.
- Rapidly cool joints, sauces, pies, etc. especially between 60°C and 20°C and then refrigerate.
- High standards of personal hygiene, especially handwashing after visiting the toilet and before handling high-risk food.
- Exclude symptomatic food handlers.
- Effective cleaning and disinfection.

Staphylococcus aureus

Sources
Human nose, mouth, skin, hands, boils, scratches, spots and cuts, especially if septic. Raw milk from cows or goats with mastitis, or products such as cheese made from raw milk. Up to 40% of the population may carry *Staphylococcus aureus* in their mouth or nose and up to 15% on their hands.

Common food vehicles
Milk and dairy products, trifles and cream desserts, custard-type products, cold cooked meat and poultry, salads, peeled cooked prawns, lasagne and fermented sausage.

Onset period
1 to 7 hours, usually 2 to 4 hours. Heat-resistant exotoxin produced in food (can survive boiling for 30 minutes). Toxic food poisoning.

SUPERVISING FOOD SAFETY (LEVEL 3) Food poisoning and foodborne disease

Symptoms and duration of illness

Abdominal pain, nausea, mainly vomiting, diarrhoea, collapse and occasionally subnormal temperatures. The duration is usually between 6 and 24 hours.

Specific characteristics

Sporadic cases may be common but are rarely notified and are not recorded. Staphylococcus multiplies in aerobic or anaerobic conditions between 7°C and 48°C. Can tolerate relatively high salt content. Usually requires millions of organisms to produce sufficient toxin to cause illness. Is usually harmless when not in food. Toxin may survive boiling for up to 30 minutes.

Specific control measures

- High standards of personal hygiene, especially handwashing before, and frequently whilst, handling high-risk food and not touching the mouth, nose or hair during food preparation.
- Avoid handling high-risk food, where possible use utensils.
- Exclude food handlers with respiratory infections especially those involving coughing or sneezing; boils or septic cuts; or skin infections that encourage scratching or flaking.
- Avoid consuming raw milk or products made from raw milk.
- Prevent cross-contamination (it may be present on chicken skin).
- Cover cuts with waterproof dressings.
- Strict temperature control of high-risk food.
- Pre-cool salad ingredients.

Bacillus cereus

Sources

Cereals, especially rice, cornflour, dried food, spices, dust, vegetation, soil and intestinal tract of humans.

Common food vehicles

Reheated rice, cornflour products, foods containing spices, vanilla slices, custards, cream pastries, soups, vegetable dishes, meats and starchy foods, e.g. pasta and potatoes.

Onset period

Usually 1 to 6 hours. Exotoxin in food, which can survive temperatures of 126°C for up to 1.5 hours. Toxic food poisoning.

Symptoms and duration of illness

Nausea, vomiting, abdominal pain and some diarrhoea. The duration is usually 12 to 24 hours.

Specific characteristics

Bacillus cereus is a spore former, which produces an exotoxin in food and multiplies under aerobic or anaerobic conditions. Both the spores and the exotoxin will survive normal cooking temperatures. Millions of organisms are usually required to cause illness and bacteria multiply between 5°C and 48°C with an optimum between 28°C and 35°C. There is a second type of *Bacillus cereus*, which resembles *Clostridium perfringens* in that it produces a toxin in the intestine. The onset period is 6 to 24 hours and symptoms are primarily abdominal pain and diarrhoea with some vomiting and fever.

Specific control measures
- Rapidly cool cooked food and store under refrigeration.
- Cooking must be thorough and, if unavoidable, reheating should be carried out at least to 75°C. Eat immediately or hot hold above 63ºC.
- Particular care with rice which should never be reheated more than once.
- Avoid cross-contamination.

Clostridium botulinum

Sources
Soil, vegetables, intestinal tract of fish and mammals.

Common food vehicles
Low-acid processed food, vacuum packed meat or fish, smoked or fermented fish, bottled vegetables, products containing spices, garlic oil, mascarpone cheese and dried milk.

Onset period
Two hours to eight days but usually 12 to 36 hours. A heat-sensitive neurotoxin produced in the food. (Affects the nervous system). Toxic food poisoning.

Symptoms and duration of illness
Difficulties in swallowing, talking and breathing. Double vision and muscular paralysis. Diarrhoea at first, followed by constipation. Fatalities are common and survivors may take several months to recover.

Specific characteristics
Clostridium botulinum multiplies between 3.3°C and 50°C under anaerobic conditions. Heat resistant spores are produced and the safety of canned food is based on the destruction of these spores, i.e. 121°C for a minimum of three minutes (botulinum cook).

Specific control measures
- Prevent post-process contamination of cans or vacuum packs of low-acid food.
- Ensure time/temperature combinations used in canning will destroy any spores of *Clostridium botulinum* that may be present.
- Do not use blown cans or cans with badly damaged seams.
- Use of preservatives such as nitrite in vacuum packs of meat.
- Thorough cooking of food immediately prior to consumption will probably destroy any toxin that is in the food.

SUPERVISING FOOD SAFETY (LEVEL 3) **Food poisoning and foodborne disease**

- Smoked fish should be produced in accordance with good manufacturing practices and preferably stored in a freezer to prevent multiplication and toxin production.
- Strict attention to the shelf life of vacuum packs.
- Strict temperature control.

Generic control measures for most food poisoning organisms

- High standards of personal hygiene, especially handwashing and exclusion of symptomatic food handlers.
- Keep raw food and high-risk food separate at all stages of production, from delivery through to service. Prevent cross-contamination.
- Store high-risk foods below 5°C or above 63°C. Cool food rapidly and keep it out of the danger zone.
- Ensure food is thoroughly cooked to core temperatures above 75°C.
- Ensure effective cleaning and disinfection.
- Ensure effective pest control.
- Avoid consuming raw foods likely to be contaminated with food poisoning organisms, especially bivalves, milk and eggs.
- Implementation of HACCP.
- The effective food safety training of all persons who can influence food safety, especially managers, supervisors and high-risk food handlers.

Food vehicles

The foods most commonly involved in food poisoning outbreaks are:
- poultry (undercooked);
- cooked red meat and meat products;
- desserts;
- shellfish (usually raw) and fish (scombrotoxin);
- salads, vegetables and fruit (usually low infective dose organisms);
- raw or undercooked egg products such as mayonnaise, mousse, and home-made ice cream; and
- milk (usually raw) and milk products.

CAUSAL FACTORS RELATING TO OUTBREAKS OF FOOD POISONING

- Preparation too far in advance and storage at ambient temperature.
- Inadequate cooling.
- Undercooking.
- Cross-contamination.
- Improper warm holding.
- Use of leftovers.
- Contaminated processed food including canned.
- Inadequate reheating.
- Inadequate thawing.
- Raw food consumed.
- Infected food handlers.
- Extra-large quantities prepared.

SUPERVISING FOOD SAFETY (LEVEL 3) Food poisoning and foodborne disease

More recently, Dr Richard North has been investigating the 'failure of management' as the most important reason for food poisoning, for example:

- failure to carry out a risk-assessment when there is a change of menu, ingredients or recipes;
- lack of contingency planning, for example, when the oven or refrigerator breaks down;
- communication – a failure of management, or head office, to provide the front-line staff with the correct information;
- management disincentives, for example, bonus paid in relation to the amount spent on cleaning or training;
- commercially driven misuse of equipment or premises, for example, overloading refrigerators or catering for numbers beyond the capacity;
- a failure to recognize potentially hazardous procedures of the operation, for example, colour-coded equipment all being washed in the same sink with no disinfection;
- failure to implement recommendations, following an earlier outbreak;
- failure to replace complex or time-consuming operations, for example, refrigerators positioned a considerable distance from workstations. This militates against small amounts of food being prepared, which results in temperature abuse;
- unrealistic demands placed on junior management or untrained staff; and
- the absence of routine planning and consistent procedures.

FOOD POISONING OUTBREAKS DEMONSTRATING MANAGEMENT FAILURES
Staphylococcus aureus

Ten people developed symptoms after eating rolls filled with egg mayonnaise. Three people were admitted to hospital. The filling had been made from hard-boiled eggs. After chopping, these eggs had been left overnight in a refrigerator which had been too warm, as a result of loss of refrigerant. The filled rolls had then been placed in a 'refrigerated' display counter which was non-operative, the ambient temperature being 25°C. The source of the outbreak was the food handler who had prepared the eggs while suffering from a skin infection. Although a 'classic' outbreak involving contamination from a food handler and inadequate temperature control, the underlying cause was the lack of equipment maintenance. This contributed significantly to the outbreak. Management also failed to recognize the hazards of inadequate temperature control and failed to realise that a food handler with a skin condition could present a serious hazard.

Salmonella

A hospital outbreak resulted in the death of three people and 119 cases of food poisoning. The vehicle of infection was roast lamb which had been cooked the day before it was served and had been left covered with cloths in a hospital corridor because of the 'sultry evening'. Conditions were considered 'absolutely perfect for bacterial multiplication'. The total consignment of 25 joints of lamb had been pre-cooked because the ovens were being repaired the following day. The hospital refrigerators were not used because they were full of jellies which would not have set at room temperature. The coroner was 'satisfied' this was an isolated incident, when someone had not 'gone by the book'. At some stage the roast lamb had become contaminated and there had been a 'classic' failure of temperature control. However, the underlying cause was clearly the failure of management to plan for the contingency of the oven repairs and to make satisfactory alternative arrangements.

Clostridium perfringens

In a hospital outbreak, patients in one of six wards who were served with roast meat and gravy succumbed to *Clostridium perfringens* food poisoning. Unaccountably, none of the patients in the other wards suffered, even though they had apparently been served the same meal. On investigation, however, it transpired that the chef had run out of gravy towards the end of serving and had quickly made up additional stock from the stock pot, without having had time to cook the mixture thoroughly. Further investigation showed that ingredient planning had been deficient in that there had been no specific quantities set out for a given number of meals. Quantities prepared were left to the judgement of the chef who estimated what was needed on an ad hoc basis. There were no established procedures, written or otherwise.

Clostridium botulinum

In June 1989 a botulism outbreak affected 27 people and one person died. The implicated product was hazelnut yoghurt. The contamination was traced to the manufacturer of canned hazelnut purée used in the yoghurt. The manufacturer was more used to producing high-acid fruit purées, in which the acidity from the fruit suppressed the growth of botulinum bacteria. However, he had employed the same process to make hazelnut purée. But this was a low-acid product, presenting a completely different order of risk. Changes to the ingredients were also made. Before the recipe had been changed, a full risk assessment should have been carried out.

Chemical food poisoning

Some chemicals are extremely poisonous and if ingested may result in a burning sensation in the mouth, severe vomiting and abdominal pain within a few minutes and occasionally diarrhoea. Chemicals can enter foodstuffs by leakage, spillage or other accidents during processing or preparation. Unacceptable levels of benzene migration from plastic packaging and inappropriate use of fungicides have resulted in poisoning. However, acute chemical poisoning from food premises is rare and is usually caused by negligence, for example, storing weedkiller, pesticide or cleaning chemicals in unlabelled food containers.

Chemical additives of food have to undergo rigorous tests before they are allowed and are usually harmless. However, some may cause problems if ingested in large amounts, for example, three persons became ill after consuming sausages containing sodium nitrate and sodium nitrite at levels of 200 times that permitted for cured meats. Symptoms included drowsiness, dizziness and a greying colour of the skin.

Residues of drugs, pesticides and fertilizers may be present in deliveries of raw materials. Pesticides sprayed onto fruit and vegetables just prior to harvesting may result in cumulative toxic effects and should be strictly controlled. Approximately 20,000 Spanish people became ill after using olive oil sold by street vendors, which allegedly contained industrial waste oil. At least 350 people died.

Metallic food poisoning

Several metals are toxic and if ingested in sufficient quantities can give rise to food poisoning. The symptoms, mainly vomiting and abdominal pain, usually develop within an hour. Diarrhoea may also occur. Metals may be absorbed by growing crops, or contaminate food during processing. Acid foods, such as fruit, should not be cooked or stored in equipment containing: antimony (enamel coatings); cadmium (refrigeration apparatus); copper (pans); lead (ceramics, earthenware and lead crystal) or zinc (galvanized metals). Soft water may absorb lead from old pipes.

Tin and Iron

Acid foods may also cause problems if stored in tin-plated iron cans for too long. The acid foods react with the tin-plate and hydrogen gas is produced. Iron and tin are absorbed by the food which may become unfit for human consumption.

Poisonous plants

Poisonous plants are rarely the cause of food poisoning in food premises. Plants responsible for causing acute poisoning include deadly nightshade, death cap (which may be mistaken for edible mushroom) daffodil bulbs and rhubarb leaves.

Red kidney beans or haricot beans which are consumed raw or undercooked occasionally result in food poisoning. Beans should be boiled for at least 10 minutes and long, slow cooking is not recommended. Nausea, vomiting and abdominal pain are likely within one to six hours of consuming the beans. Temperatures of canning will destroy the toxin.

Poisonous fish

The gonads, liver and intestines of some fish are highly toxic, for example, the puffer fish. Several incidents of red whelk poisoning have been recorded in the UK, due to a poison present in the salivary glands of these whelks. Symptoms include tingling of the fingers, disturbance of vision, paralysis, nausea, vomiting, diarrhoea and prostration.

Scombrotoxic fish poisoning

Scombrotoxic fish poisoning is caused by toxins which accumulate in the body of some fish, including tuna, mackerel, sardines, pilchards, herring, anchovies and salmon, during storage, especially above 4°C. The onset period is between ten minutes and three hours. Symptoms last up to eight hours and include headache, nausea, vomiting, abdominal pain, a rash on the face and neck, a burning or peppery sensation in the mouth, sweating and diarrhoea. Problems arise in canning fish as, once formed, the toxin is very heat-resistant and will not be destroyed during processing. Refrigerated storage of fish should prevent toxin formation.

Paralytic shellfish poisoning (PSP) and diarrhetic shellfish poisoning (DSP)

PSP and DSP may result from the consumption of mussels and other bivalves which have fed on poisonous plankton. The aquatic biotoxins causing PSP and DSP may withstand cooking. Symptoms of PSP include a tingling or numbness of the mouth almost immediately and this spreads to the neck, arms and legs within four to six hours. Death, when it does occur, is usually caused by respiratory paralysis within two to twelve hours. DSP symptoms include nausea, vomiting, abdominal pain, diarrhoea and chills with an onset time of thirty minutes to twelve hours.

FOODBORNE DISEASES (ILLNESS)

Foodborne diseases are caused by low-dose pathogens and may be considered to differ from food poisoning in that:
- a relatively small number of organisms is capable of causing the illness;
- the food acts purely as a vehicle and the multiplication of the organism within the food is not an important feature of the illness;
- vehicles other than food may transmit the organism via the faecal-oral route;
- person-to-person spread and airborne transmission is more likely; and
- the incubation period is usually longer.

Viral gastroenteritis

Viruses are present in the vomit of ill persons and viral gastroenteritis is primarily spread by airborne infection, environmental contamination and from person to person. Re-infection frequently occurs. Outbreaks involving children and closed communities are common, for example, nurseries, nursing homes, schools and cruises.

Noroviruses are the major cause of viral foodborne cases and outbreaks in the UK. The onset period is 10 to 50 hours, but usually around 24 to 48 hours, and is dose dependent. The infective dose is very low, between 10 and 100 organisms. Symptoms include vomiting, the predominant symptom and usually projectile, some diarrhoea, abdominal pain, fever and nausea. Symptoms usually last around 12 to 60 hours and patients are infectious for a further two days.

Viruses are around 3/100ths the size of bacteria and can only be seen through an electron microscope. They multiply in living cells not in food. Transmission depends on contamination of food by food handlers or sewage. Filter feeding bivalves, such as oysters harvested from sewage-polluted waters, are a major problem. Foods which are handled the most present the greatest risk; ice, desserts, cold meats, salads and some fruits are frequently involved, but the vehicle is rarely identified.

Viruses thrive in cold conditions and are destroyed at temperatures above 60°C. Relaying of shellfish in clean water is ineffective against viral contamination.

Control measures include staff training, the exclusion of ill food handlers, the implementation of HACCP, effective cleaning and disinfection of surfaces and equipment, the use of reputable suppliers and the washing/blanching of fruit and salads.

Typhoid and paratyphoid fever

Sometimes known as enteric fever, typhoid is caused by the bacterium *Salmonella* Typhi and paratyphoid by the bacterium *Salmonella* Paratyphi. The incubation period is usually between 8 and 14 days. Symptoms include fever, malaise, slow pulse, spleen enlargement, rose spots on the trunk and constipation or severe diarrhoea. The fatality rate for typhoid is between 2% and 10%. Paratyphoid is generally much less severe and symptoms may be similar to food poisoning caused by salmonella.

The organism is excreted in the faeces and urine of patients and carriers. Enteric fever may be waterborne, due to contamination by sewage, or foodborne, for example, milk or cooked meat contaminated by polluted water or by carriers who are food handlers. Laboratory confirmation is by bacteriological examination of blood, faeces or urine.

Control measures

- Using approved suppliers.
- Ensuring the safety of all water supplies. Water used for food preparation or drinking should be chlorinated.
- Ensuring the satisfactory disposal of sewage.
- Ensuring the heat treatment of milk and milk products, including ice cream.
- Preventing the sale of raw shellfish from sewage-polluted waters.
- Identifying carriers and ensuring that they are not employed within the food industry. Medical questionnaires should be used as an aid to recruitment.
- Maintaining high standards of personal hygiene amongst food handlers, especially with regard to thorough handwashing after visiting the toilet.
- Ensuring high standards of hygiene in food production and distribution.
- Washing/blanching of fruits and vegetables.

Dysentery

In the UK, bacillary dysentery is usually caused by the bacterium *Shigella sonnei*. It is an acute disease of the intestine characterized by diarrhoea, fever, stomach cramps, nausea, and often vomiting. Stools may contain blood, mucus and pus. Fatality is normally less than 1%. The incubation period is usually 1 to 3 days, although it varies between one and seven days. Dysentery is spread through faecal-oral transmission from an infected person or by the consumption of contaminated foods, including water and milk. Control measures are similar to those used for typhoid, with the emphasis on personal hygiene.

Campylobacter enteritis

Campylobacter jejuni is now the most frequently reported reason for acute bacterial diarrhoea in the UK. In 2005, around 46,000 faecal specimens submitted to laboratories in England and Wales tested positive for campylobacter and 4,581 in Scotland. However, high-risk food was only proven to be a vehicle for a few of these. The main vehicle has yet to be identified.

Symptoms include headache, fever, diarrhoea (often bloodstained), persistent colicky abdominal pain (may mimic acute appendicitis) and nausea (vomiting is rare). The incubation period is usually between two and five days and the normal duration of illness is one to seven days.

Campylobacters disappear from the stools within a few weeks of illness and long-term carriers have not been detected. Animals and wild birds are the main source and as campylobacters can survive in water for several weeks, untreated water is a potential source. Campylobacters are commonly found on raw poultry, in raw milk and sewage and on carcase meat and offal.

Transmission is thought to be from raw and undercooked poultry and meat, raw milk, bottled milk pecked by birds, especially magpies, contaminated water (private supplies) and infected dogs and cats. Person-to-person spread and secondary cases are rare. Cross-contamination from raw poultry is extremely likely and hands can carry campylobacters for up to an hour. Campylobacters multiply quickly between 37°C and 43°C but not below 28°C or above 46°C. The organisms may be destroyed by heating food to 60°C for 15 minutes and are sensitive to drying. Illness can be caused by less than 500 organisms.

Control measures include reducing the numbers of campylobacters in raw meat and the food chain, hygiene training of food handlers, especially on the dangers of cross-contamination and the importance of thorough cooking, and also raising the hygiene awareness of consumers. Milk should be heat treated and water chlorinated.

Listeriosis

Although food is not the only means of transmission, and in the majority of cases a food vehicle is not identified, listeriosis is considered to be a foodborne illness. It is caused by *Listeria monocytogenes*, which is widely distributed in the environment. It is commonly found in effluents and sewage sludge and survives many weeks after spraying. In one outbreak involving coleslaw, the cabbage, stored for several months, had been grown in a field fertilized by sheep manure. The bacteria may be excreted by human or animal carriers, and many cases of cross-infection have been recorded. Symptoms are flu-like and include fever, diarrhoea, vomiting, septicaemia, meningitis and abortion; neonates, pregnant women, immuno-suppressed persons and the elderly are most at risk. The incubation period is 1 day to 3 months. It multiplies between −1.5°C and 42°C and can multiply slowly in refrigerated foods (psychrophile).

A death rate of up to 30% is possible but mainly involves persons with other serious illness. The Government has issued warnings to at-risk groups to avoid soft cheeses, cook-chill meals and pâté, although small numbers of listeria can be found in most foods from time to time.

Escherichia coli O157

Most *E. coli* that are found in the intestine are harmless. However, *E. coli* O157 produces a powerful toxin and causes serious illness, which is sometimes fatal, particularly in young children and the elderly. Symptoms vary from a watery diarrhoea, nausea and abdominal pain to bright red bloody diarrhoea and severe abdominal cramps, usually without fever. Up to 30% of patients develop haemolytic uraemic syndrome (HUS). This generally involves young children and *E. coli* O157 is the major cause of acute renal failure in children in the UK. Fatality rates range from 1% to 5%, but in some outbreaks, for example, involving the elderly, may be much higher. The incubation period is 1 to 8 days, usually 3 to 4 days. The duration of illness is approximately two weeks, unless complications, such as HUS, develop. *E. coli* O157 disappears from adult faeces within a few days.

Although *E. coli* O157 can multiply in food, it has a very low infective dose involving less than 100 bacteria. Infection results from eating contaminated foods, person-to-person spread and direct contact with animals, especially farm animals and their faeces. A failure to wash the hands after handling raw meat or going to the toilet increases the risk of contamination. The main food vehicles are undercooked meat products, especially burgers and mince, contaminated cooked meat, vegetables fertilized with manure and unwashed, contaminated fruit. Other foods implicated include raw milk, cheese made with unpasteurized milk and apple juice. However, because of the low infective dose, cross-contamination of many ready-to-eat foods from raw meat is likely to result in illness. The main reservoir of *E. coli* O157 is the stomach and intestines of cattle and, possibly, sheep. The source is faecal material which contaminates carcases in the slaughterhouse. It survives and multiplies in some foods between 3°C and 46°C, although numbers may decline below 3°C. It is destroyed by normal, effective cooking processes. Most outbreak investigations fail to identify a food vehicle.

Hepatitis A

Infectious hepatitis is a viral infection with an abrupt onset. Symptoms include fever, malaise, nausea, abdominal pain and later jaundice. The incubation period is 15 to 50 days and the duration one week to several months. Man is the reservoir and transmission is by the faecal-oral route. Faeces, blood and urine may be infected and can contaminate food, especially water, shellfish and milk.

Control measures are similar to those used for typhoid. A temperature of 90°C for 90 seconds will inactivate the virus.

Parasites

A parasite is a plant or animal which lives on or in another plant or animal known as the host. The parasite obtains its food from the host. They often have complicated life cycles which may involve different hosts. For example, tapeworms, such as *Taenia saginata* live in man, whereas the eggs are eaten by grazing cattle and develop in the muscle of cattle. If undercooked infected beef is eaten, the adult tapeworm develops in man. Parasites may be destroyed by cooking or by commercial freezing.

SUPERVISING FOOD SAFETY (LEVEL 3) Food poisoning and foodborne disease

Characteristics of important UK pathogens

Pathogen / Infective dose	Source	Food vehicle	Growth temperature range (°C) / optimum	Growth pH range / optimum	*Onset period / duration	Typical symptoms / Oxygen reqs.	*Additional specific controls
Bacillus cereus Toxin in food (Tf) Toxin in intestine (Ti) **Medium**	Soil, vegetation, dust and a variety of cereals, especially rice, dried foods and spices. Intestinal tract of humans.	Meats, vegetable dishes, milk, cream pastries, soups and puddings, fried, boiled or cooked rice, cornflour, vanilla slices, custards and other starchy foods e.g. potatoes and pasta	5 to 48 28 to 35	4.4 to 9.3 7	(Tf) 1 to 6 hrs 12 to 24 hrs (Ti) 6 to 24 hrs 1 to 2 days	V, A, N, D (some) A, D, V (some) F Facultative anaerobe Spore former	• Thorough cooking, hot-hold (>63°C) or rapid cooling • Storing at correct temperatures • Avoid rewarming • Avoid cross-contamination
Clostridium botulinum Toxin in food (Tf) **Very low (fatalities common)**	Soil, vegetables, intestinal tracts of fish and mammals	Low-acid processed foods, bottled vegetables, garlic oil, mascarpone cheese, dry milk, meats, smoked/fermented fish and other marine products (especially in vacuum packs)	3 to 50 20 to 30 (type E)	4.6 to 9.0 7	2 hrs to 8 days usually 12 to 36 hrs several months	Difficulties in swallowing, talking and breathing, vertigo, double-vision and paralysis of cranial nerves Anaerobic Spore former	• Strict control over processing, low-acid canned foods (pH >4.5) • Use of nitrates • Discard blown cans or those with holes or defective seams • Thorough cooking • Strict control over smoking and handling of smoked fish (store in freezer) • Care in gutting and preparing raw fish • Strict attention to the shelf life of vacuum packed food (refrigerate) • Avoid cross-contamination • Temperature control
Clostridium perfringens Toxin in intestine (Ti) **Usually high**	Soil, sediment (widespread), intestinal tracts of humans and animals/sewage, raw meat, dust and insects	Beef (especially rolled joints), turkey, pork, chicken, cooked minced meat and other meat dishes, gravy, soups, stews and sauces	10 to 52 43 to 47	5.0 to 8.9 7	4 to 24 hrs usually 8 to 12 hrs 12 to 48 hrs	A, D, V (rare) Anaerobic Spore former	• Eat immediately after cooking, store above 63°C or rapid cooling and refrigeration within 1.5 hours of reaching 63°C. Strict temp control. • Joints should not exceed a size of 2.25kg • Thorough reheating of foods • Separate raw/high-risk foods • Double-wash vegetables
Salmonella spp. Infection **Medium (low in milk and high fat foods such as chocolate)**	Water, sewage, soil, birds, insects, carriers, intestinal tracts of animals, especially poultry and swine, raw meat, eggs, milk, melons, terrapins, rodents and reptiles	Beef, turkey, pork, poultry, eggs and egg products (especially raw or lightly cooked), cheese, salads, shellfish, raw milk, melons, almonds, dried coconut, baked goods, dressings (especially mayonnaise), bean sprouts and chocolate	7 to 47 37	3.8 to 9.0 7	6 to 72 hrs usually 12 to 36 hrs Upto 10 days in low dose outbreaks 1 to 7 days	A, D, V, F, N, headache Facultative anaerobe	• Sterilization and strict control of animal foodstuff • Slaughterhouse hygiene • Safe sewage disposal and chlorination of water • Screening of carriers or suspects • Avoid products made with raw eggs and not fully cooked. Use pasteurized egg. • Separation of raw/high-risk food • Thorough thawing and cooking of frozen poultry • Avoid raw milk, use heat treated • Temperature control • Vaccination of poultry • Acidification and reduction of aw
Staphylococcus aureus Toxin in food (Ti) **Medium**	Hands, skin, throats and noses of humans, boils and cuts, raw milk from cows or goats with mastitis and skin and hides of animals	Ham, turkey, chicken, pork, roast beef, egg products, salads (e.g. egg, chicken, potato, macaroni), bakery products, cream-filled pastries, luncheon meats, milk, dairy products, lasagne and fermented sausage	7 to 48 10 to 45 (for toxin production) 37	3.8 to 10.0 7	1 to 7 hrs usually 2 to 4 hours 6 to 24 hrs	A, V (mainly), D (some), N collapse and submormal temperatures Facultative anaerobe	• Avoid handling food, use utensils • Good personal hygiene, especially regarding handwashing • Exclude handlers with respiratory infections involving coughing or sneezing • Cover cuts with waterproof dressings • Exclude persons with boils or septic cuts • Avoid the use of raw milk • Refrigeration of high-risk food • Rapid cooling, pre-cool salad ingredients

Key: V=vomiting A=abdominal pain D=diarrhoea F=fever N=nausea M=malaise * Controls in addition to effective prerequisite programmes and HACCP
Source: Working group of the former PHLS Advisory Committee on Gastrointestinal Infections Guidelines 2004.

SUPERVISING FOOD SAFETY (LEVEL 3) Food poisoning and foodborne disease

Characteristics of important UK pathogens

Pathogen Infective dose	Source	Food vehicle	Growth temperature range (°C) optimum	Growth pH range optimum	Onset period duration	Typical symptoms Oxygen reqs.	*Additional specific controls
Bacillary dysentery Shigella sonnei Shigella flexneri **Very low**	Infected person/carriers - sewage/manure, water	Contaminated foods, water, milk, salads, parsley, fruits, sandwich fillings, bakery products, e.g. cream filled pastries, and shellfish. (Faecal/oral route)	N/A	N/A	12 hours to 7 days usually 1 to 3 days **2 - 16 days**	F, A, N, V, D (may contain blood/mucus) **N/A**	• Exclusion of ill food handlers, or if close contact of case • Ensure safe water supplies • Satisfactory disposal of sewage • Heat treatment of milk • Approved suppliers • Washing/blanching of fruits and salads
Campylobacter jejuni **Low**	Soil, sewage, poultry, water, animals, raw meat and raw milk. Cats, dogs, rodents and some wild birds (ducks, geese and seagulls)	Raw milk, handling raw or eating undercooked chicken, other meats, meat products, water, bottled milk pecked by birds	28 to 46 **37 to 43**	4.9 to 9.5 **7**	1 to 10 days usually 2 to 5 days **1 to 7 days**	Headache, F, D (often bloodstained) A (colicky), N V (rare) **Obligate microaerophilic**	• Reduce contamination levels of raw meat/poultry (slaughterhouse hygiene) • Hygiene of harvesters • Washing hands after handling raw poultry/meat • Keep animals/pets out of food rooms/businesses • Avoid cross-contamination • Chlorination of water (care with irrigation) • Heat treatment of milk • Thorough cooking
Escherichia coli O157 **Very low** (fatalities especially young and elderly)	Intestinal tracts of humans and animals, sewage, animal carcases and water	Raw or rare meats and poultry, raw milk and milk products, unprocessed cheese, salads, fruit, undercooked burgers/mince, cooked meats, buffets, fruit juice and seafoods	3 to 46 **37**	4.4 to 9.5 **7**	1 to 8 days usually 3 to 4 days **2 weeks or longer**	D (watery/bloody) A, N Up to 30% develop haemolytic uraemic syndrome **Facultative anaerobe**	• Reduce contamination levels of raw meat and ready-to-eat food especially at slaughterhouses • Effective separation of raw meat and ready-to-eat food (avoid cross-contamination) • Thorough cooking of meat especially burgers and mince • Double-washing salad vegetables and ready-to-eat fruit • Heat treatment of milk/apple juice • Hygiene of harvesters
Hepatitis A (viral)	Carriers, faeces, blood, urine and water	Water, shellfish, milk, icing/pastry glazes, fruit, salad, vegetables and fruit juices Faecal/oral route	N/A	N/A	15 - 50 days **(1 week or longer)**	F, M, N, A Jaundice **N/A**	• Exclusion of ill food handlers • Ensure safe water supplies • Satisfactory disposal of sewage • Heat treatment of milk • Approved suppliers • Washing/blanching of fruits and salads
Listeria monocytogenes Probably low for immuno-compromised	Soil, sewage/effluent, water, vegetation and other environmental sources, carriers, birds and mammals	Raw milk, soft cheese, coleslaw, ice cream, raw vegetables and cooked meat, raw and undercooked poultry, raw and smoked fish, paté, jellied pork tongue, fermented sausages, salads and cook-chill products	−1.5 to 42 **30 to 37**	4.4 to 9.5 **7**	1 day to 3 months **48 to 72 hrs**	Flu-like symptoms N, V, M, F, D, septicaemia, meningitis and abortion in pregnant women **Anaerobic (microaerophilic)**	• Strict stock rotation of refrigerated food and use within date code • Pregnant women to avoid high-risk foods, especially soft cheese and paté • Thorough reheating of cook-chill foods • Avoid cross-contamination, especially in factories • Washing of ready-to-eat salads etc. • Safe sewage disposal/care with irrigation • Use of clean vehicles/crates for transport of raw vegetables

Key: V=vomiting A=abdominal pain D=diarrhoea F=fever N=nausea M=malaise * Controls in addition to effective prerequisite programmes and HACCP

SUPERVISING FOOD SAFETY (LEVEL 3) Food poisoning and foodborne disease

Characteristics of important UK pathogens

Pathogen *Infective dose*	Source	Food vehicle	Growth temperature range (°C) *optimum*	Growth pH range *optimum*	Onset period *duration*	Typical symptoms *Oxygen reqs.*	*Additional specific controls
Norovirus *Very low*	Infected person, environmental contamination (airborne spread) sewage/water	Ice, desserts, cold meats, salads, some fruit, shellfish. Faecal/oral route.	N/A	N/A	10 - 50 hrs usually 24 to 48 hours *12 - 60 hrs*	V (often projectile) D (some) A, F, N N/A	• Exclusion of ill food handlers • Approved suppliers • Washing/blanching of fruits and salads • Environmental decontamination of public areas
Typhoid (*Salmonella Typhi*) **Paratyphoid - *salmonella paratyphi* Low (some fatalities)	Carriers, sewage/manure, water	Water, milk, cooked meat, dairy products, coconut, salad dressings, salads, some fruit and vegetables (manure). (Faecal/oral route)	N/A	N/A	3 days to 1 month usually 8 to 14 days (Paratyphoid usually shorter) *1 to 8 weeks*	F, N, M, headache. Rose spots on trunk. Slow pulse. Anorexia, Spleen enlargement. Constipation or sometimes D (severe) N/A	• Exclusion of ill food handlers • Ensure safe water supplies • Satisfactory disposal of sewage • Heat treatment of milk • Approved suppliers • Exclude carriers • Washing/blanching of fruits and salads • Hygiene for harvesters

Key: V=vomiting A=abdominal pain D=diarrhoea F=fever N=nausea M=malaise * Controls in addition to effective prerequisite programmes and HACCP
** Paratyphoid is less severe and symptoms may be similar to salmonella food poisoning.

5 Personal hygiene

High standards of personal hygiene are essential to prevent contamination of food and food poisoning. Food safety legislation requires:

- every person working in a food-handling area to maintain a high standard of personal cleanliness, including wearing suitable, clean and, where appropriate, protective clothing;
- the supervision and instruction and/or training of food handlers in food hygiene matters commensurate with their work activity; and
- persons known or suspected to be suffering from, or carriers of, a disease likely to be transmitted through food, including infected wounds, skin infections or diarrhoea, must be excluded from food handling if there is a likelihood of contaminating food with pathogenic organisms.

Supervisors involved in interviewing potential food handlers should ensure they are smart and clean, free of skin infections and have no health problems which could expose food to risk of contamination. Hands should be clean, nails short and not be bitten. They should demonstrate a good attitude towards hygiene, a willingness to undergo training and not wear excessive jewellery or make-up.

Food handlers must have high standards of personal hygiene.

Training of food handlers

Training involves the provision of knowledge and its implementation (practice) to ensure proficiency. Food handlers need to understand the controls, monitoring and corrective actions to be taken at points critical to food safety for which they are responsible. Thus food handlers involved with high-risk food preparation require more training than those handling only packaged or low-risk foods.

Food businesses require a planned training programme which includes induction, awareness and continuous refresher training. The knowledge provided will depend on the risks and responsibilities associated with each job. Knowledge may be provided by instruction, attending in-house or formal courses or from computer programmes. However, to be successful it is essential that there is commitment and support from directors and managers, effective supervision and adequate resources. High standards of food safety result when the culture of the business ensures good hygiene practices are implemented and rewarded.

Hazards from food handlers

Potential hazards arise from *Staphylococcus aureus* which is often present on the hands, in the nose or mouth and in spots and septic cuts. Cross-contamination is also probable if hands are not properly washed after touching raw meat, or other contaminated sources, before handling high-risk foods. A very serious hazard is presented if food handlers fail to wash their hands after using the toilet. The faecal-

SUPERVISING FOOD SAFETY (LEVEL 3) Personal hygiene

oral route is one of the main ways that low-dose pathogens (those organisms which only require a few to be present on food to make you ill), such as *E. coli* O157, *Shigella sonnei* or *campylobacter* result in illness. Persons with loose stools and carriers may be responsible for several serious outbreaks of foodborne illness because of poor personal hygiene.

Hands

Hands are the main vehicle for transferring food poisoning bacteria to high-risk food. For this reason, hands should be kept clean and washed frequently throughout the day and especially:

- after visiting the toilet (toilet paper is porous);
- on entering the food room, after a break, and before handling any food or equipment;
- after dealing with an ill customer or a baby's nappy;
- between handling raw food, such as poultry, red meat, eggs or shellfish, and handling ready-to-eat food;
- after changing or putting on a dressing;
- after cleaning up animal faeces (guide dog or guard dog) or handling boxes contaminated with bird droppings;
- after combing or touching the hair, nose, mouth or ears;
- after eating, smoking, coughing or blowing the nose;
- after handling external packaging or flowers;
- after handling waste food or refuse; and
- after cleaning, or handling dirty cloths, crockery etc.

The correct handwashing procedure is essential. Around 3 to 5ml of liquid soap should be applied to wet hands. A good lather should be produced by rubbing the hands and fingertips together. Between the fingers, around the thumbs and wrists should be thoroughly lathered for about 20 seconds. Special attention should be paid to the fingertips and nails. The lather should be rinsed off in warm flowing water at around 43°C. Efficient drying of the hands with a clean disposable paper towel will reduce the number of bacteria even more. A paper towel may be used to turn off the tap. Sufficient lather, friction and warm running water are the essential features to removing transient bacteria from the hands. Some warm air driers are very slow which results in staff leaving the toilet with wet hands or drying them on their protective clothing. Furthermore, unlike paper towels, driers do not remove bacteria from the hands.

A soft nailbrush must be used to remove bacteria from the fingertips and under the fingernails after using the toilet, cleaning up vomit or faecal material, changing a dressing or handling raw poultry or meat before handling high-risk food. Excessive use of a stiff nailbrush and bactericidal soap both increase the risk of dermatitis. Gloves are often defective or abused and not necessary in most food handling situations. If disposable gloves are used in very high-risk situations the hands should be washed before putting on the gloves and after taking them off. The gloves should be discarded frequently and immediately if damaged.

As fingernails may harbour dirt and bacteria, they must be kept short and clean. False nails should not be worn. Nail varnish may chip and contaminate food and should not be used. Persons who continually put their fingers in their mouth, for example, nail-biters should not be employed as food handlers because of the risk of contaminating food with *Staphylococcus aureus*.

As far as practicable, the best policy is to avoid handling food by using hygienic utensils and equipment, such as serving tongs, trays and plates which are carried by the rim. Furthermore, the hands should not come into contact with the parts of the glasses, cups, spoons, etc. that will end up in a customer's mouth.

The nose, mouth and ears

Up to 40% of adults carry *Staphylococcus aureus* in their nose. Coughs and sneezes can carry droplet infection for considerable distances and contaminate food and/or work surfaces. Persons with bad colds or continuously coughing and sneezing should not handle open food. Hands should be washed after blowing the nose and single-use disposable paper handkerchiefs are preferred. Food handlers preparing food who need to cough or sneeze immediately, should turn away from the food and cough/sneeze into their upper arm. As the upper arm is unlikely to come into contact with food or food-contact surfaces this should minimize any risk of contamination.

As the mouth is also likely to harbour *Staphylococcus aureus*, food handlers should not eat sweets, chew gum, taste food with fingers or a previously used spoon, or blow into glasses to polish them. Spitting is obviously prohibited as is nose and teeth picking or poking fingers into the ears. All of these practices transfer bacteria to food directly or indirectly.

Discharges from the ears, eyes and nose may contaminate food and such ailments must be reported to the supervisor. Medical clearance will normally be required before resuming work. Effective supervision, clear instruction and training are essential to minimize hazards from the nose, mouth and ears.

Cuts, boils, septic spots and skin infections

Food handlers with boils and septic lesions should be excluded from high-risk food-handling areas as they will be infected with *Staphylococcus aureus*. If a cut occurs at work it should be cleaned, disinfected and dried, then completely protected with a conspicuously coloured waterproof dressing. Blue dressings are used to improve their visibility in food if they fall off. Loose dressings should be replaced immediately. Loss of dressings must be reported immediately to the supervisor. Cuts at work should be entered in the accident book.

Cuts on hands may need the extra protection of waterproof finger-stalls. Waterproof dressings are necessary to prevent blood and bacteria contaminating the food and to prevent bacteria from food, especially raw meat or fish, infecting the wound which may turn septic. Furthermore, waterproof dressings do not collect grease and dirt. Metal strips incorporated in dressings assist detection only where metal detectors are in use. Staff must not scratch or pick spots or cuts.

Staff who report for work wearing unacceptable dressings must have them changed before they enter a food room or commence food-handling duties.

First aid

Food businesses must have a suitable and sufficient supply of first-aid materials. One person should be given the responsibility of ensuring adequate provisions are always available. It is advisable to have at least one person trained in first aid and this may be a legal requirement.

The hair

Hair is constantly falling out and, along with dandruff, can result in contamination of food products by bacteria, especially *Staphylococcus aureus*. The hair should be shampooed regularly, tied back if long and preferably completely enclosed by suitable head covering. Hairnets worn under hats and helmets are recommended. Combing of hair and adjustment of head covering should only take place in cloakrooms and should not be carried out whilst wearing protective clothing, as hairs may end up on the shoulders and then in the food. Hair grips and clips may also contaminate food and should never be worn outside the head covering. Scratching of the head should be avoided.

Jewellery and perfume

Food handlers should not wear earrings, watches, jewelled rings or brooches as they harbour dirt and bacteria and restrict effective handwashing (microbiological hazard). Furthermore, stones and small pieces of metal are a potential physical hazard. They may end up in the food and result in a customer complaint. Strong-smelling perfume, handcreams or aftershave are a potential chemical hazard and should not be worn by the food handlers as they may taint the food, especially food with a high fat content. Most food businesses allow staff to wear a plain wedding ring and a sleeper earring. Body piercings in exposed parts of the body are unacceptable and at the very least require covering with a suitable plaster.

Smoking

Smoking and the use of tobacco is prohibited in food rooms or whilst handling open food because:

- ♦ of the danger of contaminating food from fingers which touch the lips and may transfer bacteria to food;
- ♦ cigarette ends contaminated with saliva are placed on working surface;
- ♦ cigarette ends and ash may contaminate the food;
- ♦ it encourages coughing; and

Notices should not be ignored

♦ an unpleasant environment may be created for non-smokers.

Legible notices should be displayed instructing food handlers who need to smoke to use specified locations and never to smoke in the food rooms. It is illegal to smoke in any enclosed public place in Scotland. After smoking, food handlers should wash their hands.

Protective clothing

All food handlers and visitors should wear clean, washable, light-coloured, easy-to-clean protective clothing, preferably without external pockets. Pockets are used for keeping pens, sweets, handkerchiefs and cigarettes. All of which could expose food to risk of contamination. Press studs or Velcro fastening are preferable to buttons. Protective garments should be appropriate for the work being carried out and should completely cover ordinary clothing. Jumper and shirt sleeves must not protrude and, if short-sleeved overalls are worn, only clean forearms must be visible. Staff must be aware that protective clothing is primarily worn to protect the food from risk of contamination and not to keep their own clothes clean. Outdoor clothing and personal effects must not be brought into food rooms. Dust, pet hairs and woollen fibres are just a few of the contaminants carried on ordinary clothing. Lockers for outdoor clothing should be provided in non-food rooms.

The correct procedure must always be followed when putting on protective clothing. Head covering should always be put on first, followed by coats or boiler suits to avoid hairs getting on to the shoulders of protective clothing. Protective head covering should not be removed at breaks unless the protective overall or coat is removed first. Protective clothing should not be kept in toilets and, if practical, should be removed prior to using the toilet. Protective clothing should not be worn outside the food premises, not used to travel to and from work and not worn during lunch time sporting activities such as football or lying on the grass.

The use of different coloured protective clothing is recommended to distinguish between staff who handle only raw food and those who handle high-risk food. In addition, disposable protective clothing is becoming more widely available.

Aprons, if worn, should be suitable for the particular operation, light-coloured and capable of being thoroughly cleaned or disposable. Aprons which are torn or have badly-worn surfaces which create cleaning difficulties should be replaced. Facilities should be provided for cleaning waterproof aprons at various times during production and at the end of each working day.

Cleanable hooks should be provided for hanging up aprons.

Dirty or soiled protective clothing, exposes food to risk of contamination and must be replaced. A system, of which staff are aware, must be in place to ensure clean protective clothing is available when required. Dirty protective clothing should be laundered so there is no risk to food. Suitable footwear should be worn to prevent slipping and to protect the feet. Boots may be provided for wearing in wet areas. They should be anti-slip, unlined and easy to clean. Suitable facilities should be provided for cleaning and storing cleaned boots.

Exclusion of food handlers

Supervisors must be aware that apparently healthy, symptom-free employees may be carriers of, and excrete, pathogenic bacteria. Laboratory testing cannot be relied on to detect small numbers of intermittently excreted pathogens. High standards of hygiene are therefore the only way to prevent the contamination of food by an infected food handler. It is a legal requirement for food handlers to advise their supervisor if they are suffering from diarrhoea or vomiting and/or suspect they may be carrying a food poisoning organism.

Food handlers with food poisoning symptoms, such as diarrhoea or vomiting, or suspected of carrying foodborne organisms, e.g. because of close contact with a confirmed case of typhoid or consuming a meal known to have caused illness, must be excluded from any job which would expose food to risk of contamination. Where appropriate, the Environmental Health Department should be informed immediately so that an environmental health practitioner/officer can carry out urgent investigations. The guidance from the Department of Health, 'Food Handlers: Fitness to Work' states that any person who is excreting food poisoning organisms must not be allowed to engage in food handling until they have been free of symptoms for 48 hours, once any treatment has ceased, and have received medical clearance. However, it is critical that good hygiene, particularly handwashing, is observed. Food handlers suffering from typhoid or paratyphoid must provide six consecutive negative faecal specimens, after treatment, before they can resume food handling duties.

If the supervisor has no confidence in the hygiene standards of a food handler who is a carrier of a food poisoning organism, even when symptom-free for 48 hours, they should not be allowed to handle high-risk food.

Food handlers returning from holidays abroad, particularly from countries with warm climates and suspect sanitation, should complete a short medical questionnaire. Even if they have fully recovered from symptoms of diarrhoea or vomiting experienced on holiday, they should be excluded from food handling until they have provided at least one negative specimen. Food handlers without symptoms of food poisoning could be allowed to undertake non-food handling jobs until clearance is received. They should be closely supervised and observe the highest standards of handwashing.

Food handlers with skin infections such as psoriasis, boils or septic cuts, respiratory tract infections, infection of the eyes or ears, dental sepsis or purulent gingivitis must also be excluded until medical clearance has been obtained.

Visitors

Visitors to food businesses should be closely supervised to ensure that they do not expose food to risk of contamination. They should wear clean protective clothing and observe all personal hygiene rules applying to staff.

Visitors with food poisoning symptoms or any other conditions which would result in the exclusion of a food handler, should not be allowed in the food room.

The role of the supervisor in personal hygiene

Effective supervision is essential to ensure high standards of personal hygiene. Supervisors must lead by example, especially in relation to handwashing and wearing protective clothing. They should ensure the appropriate facilities are provided and that soap, paper towels and protective clothing are always available. Supervisors should provide clear instruction and training and monitor staff to ensure rules are adhered to. Posters and notices may be provided. Mistakes should be corrected and staff motivated to observe the highest standards. Glo-Germ or hand swabs may prove useful. Staff who deliberately or consistently flout hygiene rules should be disciplined.

Key points

- Most food handlers will carry food poisoning organisms at one time or another.
- High standards of personal hygiene are essential to avoid contamination of food.
- Hygiene training of food handlers will assist in the prevention of food poisoning.
- Frequent handwashing is essential.
- Cuts should be protected with brightly coloured waterproof dressings.
- Food should be handled as little as possible.
- Food handlers who are suffering from or are suspected of carrying infections, which may contaminate food, should be excluded until medical clearance has been received.

6 The storage and temperature control of food

The storage of food is important to ensure adequate provision throughout the year and to overcome fluctuations in supply. However, failure to ensure satisfactory conditions of temperature, humidity, stock rotation and the integrity of packaging can result in problems of unfit or spoiled food and will, at the very least, result in a considerable reduction in shelf life. Inadequate temperature control is the most common cause of food poisoning. Correct storage and good temperature control is therefore crucial to food safety.

Delivery and unloading of raw materials

An effective documented checking system should be in place for selecting suppliers and dealing with deliveries. This will assist in demonstrating due diligence, should the need arise, and ensure that deliveries meet the agreed specification. Deliveries should only be accepted from approved suppliers. All deliveries should be checked before storage. The delivery vehicle should be clean and, if necessary, refrigerated. All outer packaging should be in good condition and not be discoloured or contaminated, e.g. from bird droppings. Food should be of a good quality and suitably labelled and date coded. It should have sufficient shelf life to enable it to be used. Chilled food should be delivered below 5ºC and frozen food at/or below −18ºC. Food should be checked with a calibrated probe thermometer and details recorded. Satisfactory deliveries should be moved to storage within 15 minutes of unloading. If high-risk food is delivered in an unrefrigerated vehicle, it should usually be rejected. However, in certain circumstances involving very short journeys the temperature of the food should be checked, if it is below 8ºC it may be accepted. Food from unapproved sources, unsatisfactory delivery vehicles, out of date, damaged packaging, showing evidence of pests, or chilled food above 8ºC or frozen food above −15ºC should be rejected and the supplier notified. Alternative suppliers may be required if there are serious or frequent problems and rejections. Raw food and high-risk food should be completely segregated to avoid risk of contamination. Non-food items, especially chemicals, and strong-smelling foods which may cause taint problems should normally be delivered separately. Delivery records should be completed for foods that are accepted or rejected including details of any checks undertaken, e.g. temperature. The delivery area should be kept clean and tidy and someone should always be available to accept deliveries.

Raw meat and poultry

Raw meat joints should be stored between -1˚C and +1˚C, with a relative humidity of around 90%. Joints should keep for up to a week, although processed raw meats and offals will have a shorter life. Products should not touch the wall surface. Only approved suppliers should be used.

Eggs

Raw eggs are a source of salmonella and must be handled with care. Salmonella may be present inside the egg or on the shell, especially if contaminated with chicken faeces. Retailers should store eggs at a constant cool temperature below 20ºC. Fluctuations of temperature may result in condensation on the shell and salmonella being sucked into the egg from the surface. Stock rotation is essential.

Caterers should purchase eggs from a reputable supplier. Lion-branded and date-coded eggs are preferable as they originate from hens vaccinated against salmonella. Soiled, cracked and out-of-date eggs should be rejected. The caterer should store eggs under refrigeration and use within three weeks of lay, as both of these factors will prevent the multiplication of any salmonella that may be present. Some food businesses remove eggs from refrigeration at least 30 minutes before cooking, to ensure that correct cooking temperatures are achieved.

Meat pies, pasties and sausage rolls

These products must be obtained from a reliable source and should preferably be stored under refrigeration. Temperatures of around 7°C, with good air movement, are recommended so that the pastry remains crisp. As these foods are cooked to temperatures as high as 90°C, very few bacteria survive. Consequently, they remain bacteriologically safe at higher refrigeration temperatures. However, stock rotation is important and such products should be sold on the day of production or the following day. Pies or pasties to which something has been added after baking should be stored at or below 5°C. Temperatures should be kept constant as fluctuations result in condensation and mould growth.

As these products may be consumed without further cooking they must never be stored with raw meat or vegetables. Strong-smelling foods, such as cheese, may introduce taint or mould problems. Price tickets must not be stuck into pies or any other food. If pies are to be sold hot from retail outlets they must be cooked thoroughly and, if stored, maintained above 63°C. Alternatively, pies may be microwaved as required. They must never be rewarmed.

Fruit and vegetables

Although each fruit and vegetable has its own optimal storage conditions, a general guide is to keep them in a cool room or a refrigerator. However, tropical fruits such as pineapples and bananas should be stored at 10°C to 13°C to avoid 'chill injury'. Dry stores are often used for the storage of fruit and vegetables. Care must be taken to prevent warm, moist conditions and condensation which will encourage bacterial spoilage and mould growth. Low humidities and excessive ventilation result in dehydration and must also be avoided. Fruit should be examined regularly and mouldy items removed to avoid rapid mould spread. Transit wrappings, especially 'non-breathing' plastic films, may need to be removed to avoid condensation. A stock rotation system to ensure older produce is used first, must be implemented. Fruit and vegetables, especially when served raw, are being implicated in more outbreaks of foodborne illness. Tomatoes, spinach, broccoli, lettuce, cut melon and raspberries have all been implicated in outbreaks including salmonella and *E. coli* O157. Vigorous washing, turbulence and brushing will all help to reduce the levels of bacteria as well as removing soil, dust, insects and some chemicals. Unfortunately, washing is unlikely to remove all bacteria or chemicals such as pesticides.

Ice cream

Ice cream should be kept in clean, dedicated freezers. Ice cream must not be stored with raw products. It should always be kept frozen and discarded if defrosted. Defrosted ice cream is a hazard because, if it is at a high enough temperature, it provides ideal nutrients for the growth of pathogens such as salmonella. Tubs should be used completely before fresh tubs are started and nothing should be placed on top of open tubs. Lids should normally be kept on. The texture of ice cream is more temperature sensitive than other frozen foods and it may be held at -12°C before use.

Milk and cream

Milk and cream should be stored under refrigeration (below 5°C) and should be placed in the refrigerator or cold store as soon as received. Imitation cream should also be refrigerated. Crates of milk should not be stored below raw meat.

Flour and cereals

Flour and cereals should preferably be stored in mobile stainless steel containers. Lids must be tight-fitting. Large stocks of flour kept in original sacks must be stored clear of the ground and free from damp. Condensation may result in mould growth on wet flour and must be prevented. Regular cleaning of containers used for flour storage must not be overlooked. Frequent inspections and stock rotation should be carried out to check for rodents or insects.

Canned foods

Canned foods are usually kept in a dry store which is cool, well ventilated and free from condensation. Stock rotation is important, especially cans of high-acid fruit, such as prunes, rhubarb and tomatoes which may blow if stored longer than recommended by the manufacturer. (The acid attacks the can wall, especially at the seam, to produce gas.) Cans should be inspected weekly and blown, leaking or rusty cans removed. Stock rotation is important although some cans, e.g. containing fish in oil, may keep for at least 5 years.

On opening, can contents should be placed in the refrigerator in a suitable covered container if not required for immediate use. This will avoid mould and contamination problems and shards of metal ending up in the food. Furthermore, acid food attacks the can wall and excessive amounts of tin or iron may end up in the food which is likely to develop a metallic taint.

If the food is discoloured or has an unusual smell or texture, or the interior of the can is rusty, the food should be rejected.

Some large cans of meat, especially ham, may only have been pasteurized and therefore need to be stored under refrigeration. If this is the case the can will be clearly labelled.

Wrapping and packaging

Packaging and wrapping materials must be stored in clean, dry areas where they are not exposed to risk of contamination.

Cling film

Cling film is useful for stopping food drying out and protecting it against contamination (special breathing films are available for raw meats). Under certain conditions, however, it can speed up spoilage and mould growth by trapping moisture. It is important therefore that:

- raw meat or wet food is unwrapped when removed from the refrigerator; and
- food wrapped in cling film is not left in bright light or sunlight.

Because of the risk of chemical migration, cling films should not be used where they could melt into food during heating, or for wrapping foods with a high fat content, unless manufacturer's advice indicates their suitability for this purpose.

Vacuum packing

Vacuum-packed food, and modified atmosphere packs, should be refrigerated, to prevent the multiplication of anaerobic bacteria. Immediately after opening a vacuum pack, the contents should be removed completely. Slightly darker colours of meat and the acid odour will disappear shortly after being removed.

Care must be taken to avoid puncturing packs, for example, with sharp bones or rough handling. Defective seams commonly result in the loss of pack integrity. However, air-tight vacuum packaging may blow if the contents ferment. It is advisable to purchase branded vacuum packs from reputable suppliers to avoid receiving low-grade meat of dubious origin. Unmarked packs without 'use-by' dates should always be regarded with suspicion.

Unfit food and damaged stock

All unfit or damaged stock should be segregated and thoroughly examined before use. Suspect food should be clearly marked as 'unfit' or 'not to be sold!' A suitable dustbin or container may be designated for the purpose. If there is any doubt regarding the fitness of food it should be discarded, or the local Environmental Health Department may be asked for advice. This includes food which is contaminated, spoilt, date-expired, unlabelled, temperature-abused, suspected of causing food poisoning or subject to a food alert warning.

The greenhouse effect

Food, especially high-risk food, should not be stored in windows or in glass display cabinets which are exposed to direct sunlight. The heat within the cabinet will build up in the same way that it does in a greenhouse, providing conditions ideal for bacterial multiplication. The greenhouse effect may even occur in chill cabinets without proper chilled air circulation, and fluorescent tubes may exaggerate the problem.

SUPERVISING FOOD SAFETY (LEVEL 3) **The storage and temperature control of food**

Stock rotation

Satisfactory rotation of stock, to ensure that older food is used first, is essential to avoid spoilage, food poisoning and unnecessary wastage. Stock rotation applies to all types of food. Daily checks should be made on short-life perishable food stored in refrigerators whereas weekly examination of other foods may suffice. Stock which is undisturbed for long periods will encourage pest infestations. The rule is: 'First in, first out'. Written stock control records are recommended and are useful to assist a due-diligence defence. Food should always be checked before use to ensure it is within date, in good condition and packaging is undamaged.

Codes

Stock rotation has been much easier since the advent of open-date coding but some products do not require a 'use-by' or 'best-before' date. In these cases, retailers should adopt their own code to identify the date of delivery. A colour code system is one of the easiest to use: a blue line for Monday; a red line for Tuesday; etc. A double coloured line should be used the following week. 'Use-by' dates are placed on perishable, high-risk, short-life products, whereas 'best-before' dates are used on longer life products. Products with an expired 'use-by' date should be considered as unfit, whereas those products with an expired 'best-before' date are more likely to be of an unacceptable quality. The practice of selling old stock cheaply is not recommended. It is an offence to display for sale or sell any food which is unfit or foods bearing an expired 'use-by' date or to change this date. It is not an offence to display or sell food with an expired best-before date, unless it is unfit. Food which is past its use-by date should be segregated from food intended for sale. It should be placed in a suitable container or wrapped with tape that states 'unfit' or 'not for sale' or 'date expired' etc.

Dry-goods stores

Rooms used for the storage of fruit and vegetables, dried, canned and bottled foods should be kept dry, cool (preferably between 10°C and 15°C), well lit, well ventilated and free from risk of condensation. Shelves should be easy to clean and non-absorbent. They must be kept clean and tidy and spillages should be cleared away promptly. Rodent and bird-proofing should be maintained and any gaps in the fabric should be sealed. As far as possible food should be kept in rodent-proof containers. All goods should be stored clear of walls and off the floor to allow cleaning and pest control. Stock should be rotated and inspected regularly.

Non-food items, including cleaning equipment and chemicals, and strong smelling foods should not be stored in dry-goods stores. Packs of food should be handled carefully to avoid damage. Part-used packs should be resealed to prevent contamination.

SUPERVISING FOOD SAFETY (LEVEL 3) **The storage and temperature control of food**

REFRIGERATORS

Refrigerators should be readily accessible, and sited clear of heat sources such as ovens and high-intensity lights unless they are designed for high-temperature environments. Ideally they should be in well-ventilated areas away from the direct rays of the sun. Multi-deck, open display cabinets should be sited clear of draughts from doorways, and ventilation and heating grills fitted in ceilings, which may result in significant increase in temperatures. High humidities should be avoided, as these will cause condensation on stored foods. The siting of all units should permit the cleaning of surrounding areas as well as the cooling coils. Regular maintenance and defrosting (where not automatic) should be carried out and door seals checked.

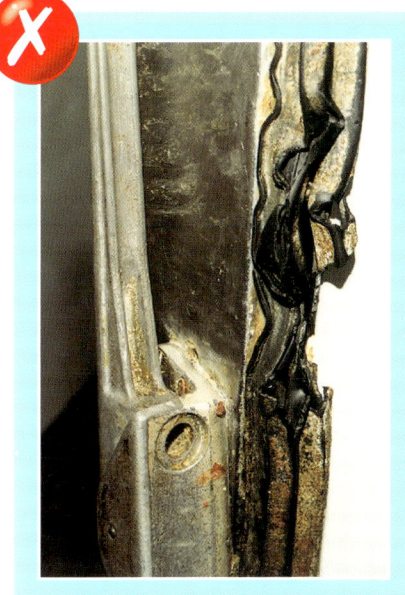

Defective refrigerator door seals should be replaced

Cleaning should be frequent, at least weekly, taking in both exteriors, especially door handles, and interiors. Internal surfaces and fans should also be disinfected. Warm water and bicarbonate of soda may be used to remove mould and yeast. Base plates and baffle plates should be removed to check for debris such as price tickets and packaging which can obstruct air flow and block drains in multi-deck units. Drip trays, if present, should be emptied and cleaned. Dust on evaporator coils and air ducts must be removed to maintain performance.

After cleaning and disinfection, units should be completely dried and brought to correct operating temperatures before being reloaded. Stock should be kept in back-up chill stores during cleaning operations.

Operating temperatures

The optimum temperature for multi-use refrigerators, in which high-risk foods are stored, is between 1°C and 4°C. Cook-chill foods with a maximum shelf life of five days must be kept between 0°C and 3°C. The maximum legal temperature for high-risk food stored in a refrigerator is 8°C. Cold food on a display buffet may rise above 8°C on one occasion for up to 4 hours.

If the dial on a refrigerator displays 12°C it should be observed for a few minutes as it may be because the door has been left open. If the display temperature drops to around 5°C then no further action is required. If the temperature remains at 12°C the contents of the refrigerator should be checked to ensure hot food or a large consignment of, for example, bottled drink at ambient temperature has been placed inside. If there is no obvious problem and the thermostat cannot be turned down the temperature of the food should be checked. If the food temperature is less than 8°C or cannot have been above 8°C for more than 4 hours it should be moved to another refrigerator and maintenance called to repair the refrigerator. If the food has been above 8°C for more than 4 hours it should be discarded.

Hot food

Hot food, not intended for immediate consumption, should be cooled rapidly. It should not be placed directly into a refrigerator as this may raise the temperature of food already stored, as well as increasing the ice build-up on the cooling unit. Condensation may also occur on some foods, resulting in an unacceptable drip on to food stored below. However, depending on the amount of food and the capacity of the refrigerator, it may be preferable to place a small amount of food which has cooled to around 50°C into a large capacity unit instead of leaving it in a warm environment for prolonged periods or overnight.

Ice build-up on the cooling unit

Contamination

It is essential that precautions are taken to avoid contamination. Raw food must always be kept apart from high-risk food. It is recommended that separate, clearly labelled units be used. If only one refrigerator is available, high-risk food must be stored above raw food. Shelves previously used for raw foods must not be used for high-risk foods without cleaning and disinfection. All foods should be adequately covered to prevent drying out, cross-contamination and the absorption of odour.

Packing and rotation of food

Refrigerators should not be overloaded and they need packing in a manner which allows good air circulation. A gap of at least 3cm should always be allowed between trays stored on slatted shelves. Food should not be placed directly in front of the cooling unit as this reduces efficiency. Non-perishables should not be stored in a refrigerator if this takes up valuable space. Good stock rotation is essential, and daily checks should be made for out-of-date stock. Stock rotation is important because of the slow growth of mould, spoilage bacteria and especially the pathogen *Listeria monocytogenes*. Particular care is required with soft cheeses and pâté which have been associated with listeria outbreaks.

Staff responsibilities

Staff should be given clear instructions on how to use refrigerators. They should open doors for as little, and for as short a time, as possible. The temperature of the refrigerator should be checked regularly and recorded at least twice a day. Records will assist a due-diligence defence. Spillages should be cleared up immediately.

The storage life of perishable food under refrigeration

Shelf life varies according to the operating temperature of the refrigerator and the specific perishable food. For example, at 1°C, most vegetables will keep for at least two weeks, butter for two months and fresh beef up to a week.

Chilled display cabinets

Cabinets should be loaded correctly so that cold air inlets are not obstructed and load-lines are not exceeded. Only chilled products should be placed in display cabinets.

Radiant heat can have a significant effect on food stored in chilled cabinets, particularly on the upper shelves. Cabinets, therefore, should be sited away from heating units and high-intensity lights and out of direct sunlight.

Monitoring temperatures

Cabinet thermometer readings should be checked using an accurate digital or infrared thermometer. Indicating or recording thermometers are essential and premises with a large number of units will need automatic monitoring equipment and alarms to warn of unacceptable temperatures. If readings indicate air temperatures above prescribed limits, then the temperature of a food simulator or between-pack temperatures should be taken. If concern remains then probing of the food should be undertaken.

Using digital probe thermometers

The use of accurate tip-sensitive thermometers is the best way to check the temperature of cold or hot food. Probes must be cleaned and disinfected before and after use, to ensure there is no risk of cross-contamination. Probes should always be cleaned before using disinfecting wipes and a contact time of 30 seconds is recommended. Alternatively, hot water above 82°C may be used to disinfect the probe. To ensure probes are accurate, they should be validated (calibrated) weekly/monthly depending on use. Validation involves using slush ice, when the temperature should read 0°C, and boiling water, when the temperature should read 100°C. Alternatively, test caps may be used. An error of up to plus or minus 1°C is acceptable.

Common mistakes involving the use of probe thermometers include:
- failing to clean and disinfect before use;
- not allowing sufficient time for an accurate reading;

SUPERVISING FOOD SAFETY (LEVEL 3) **The storage and temperature control of food**

- not taking the core temperature;
- not using a calibrated thermometer; and
- taking a false reading because the probe is touching a bone or the side of a container.

Infrared thermometers

Infrared thermometers, which work by measuring the amount of radiant energy, can be used to scan foods very rapidly. Any identified problems can be checked immediately with a digital thermometer. Additional advantages include the fact that it is non-destructive testing and there is no risk of cross-contamination. It is particularly useful for scanning retail cabinets, frozen food, deliveries and despatch as large consignments can be checked for hot spots.

Temperature data loggers

Data loggers and printers will provide a variety of useful information about refrigerated storage including current temperature, maximum, minimum and trends of temperature over a specified period. Should temperatures rise above a predetermined level they can also trigger an alarm.

Cooking

Cooking is used to make food palatable and safe for immediate consumption. Core temperatures of 75°C are usually adequate to destroy food poisoning bacteria although some preformed toxins and spores will not be destroyed. Lower temperatures for longer times may be equally effective. A disinfected digital probe thermometer should be used to check correct core temperatures have been achieved, especially for poultry and rolled joints. Colour and texture changes (no pink bits), and 'juices of poultry running clear' are useful indicators of correct cooking.

Cooked food should, unless it is immediately cooled, be kept hot at or above the legal temperature of 63ºC or served for immediate consumption. This temperature prevents the germination of spores or the multiplication of bacteria. Hot food on display in a buffet is allowed to fall below 63ºC for a maximum period on one occasion of up to 2 hours.

Microwaves are often used for cooking and reheating food. The main advantage is that cooking is quick. However, there is a danger of cold spots, if manufacturers' instructions are not followed. Bacteria will survive in these cold spots.

If bloody chicken is served to a customer this indicates undercooking. The chicken should be replaced and action taken to prevent recurrence. The usual reason for undercooked chicken is inadequate thawing time. Other reasons could be inadequate cooking time for the size of the chicken or a defective oven. Regular maintenance of the oven will reduce the likelihood of this latter problem. The temperature of the chicken should be checked after cooking to ensure 75ºC or equivalent has been achieved.

Cooling of hot food

Rapid cooling of cooked foods to be chilled or frozen is extremely important to prevent spore germination or the multiplication of any surviving pathogens or those introduced. It is usually recommended that food is cooled below 10°C in less than 1.5 hours to minimize time in the danger zone. Practically, only blast chillers can achieve this. A more pragmatic standard adopted by the Food and Drugs Authority in America is to cool joints from 60°C to 21°C in two hours and from 21°C to 7°C within a further four hours. Ice water baths cool faster than cold air.

Large quantities of liquids such as gravies and stews which are intended for reheating, create ideal conditions for anaerobic spore-forming bacteria to cause problems. Cooking activates the spores which germinate during long, slow cooling. Large numbers of vegetative bacteria may be produced and mild rewarming will not destroy them. Food poisoning is likely. Cool spots may occur during cooking or reheating because of the volume of liquid, the use of large, tall pans, absence of lids, failure to stir and the base of the pan being bigger than the heat source. Even though the surface of the liquid may be boiling uneven heat distribution sets up currents which generate cool spots where bacteria may survive and even multiply.

When cooling food, the following basic rules should be applied:
- minimize bulk – the smaller the size of the food, the faster it will cool. The maximum joint size recommended is usually 2·5kg;
- maximize surface area – square or rectangular containers present greater surface areas than round containers. Shallow containers should be used instead of deep containers;
- maximize differential – the greater the difference in temperatures between the product and its surroundings, the faster it will cool; and
- air flow from a fan about 10cm from the food will increase heat transfer by a factor of 3 (food should be covered).

Although there is a potential hazard if joints of meat are cooled too slowly, the risk may be smaller than that from post-cooking contamination, e.g. slicing with a dirty knife.

Hot food must be completely cooled before wrapping in impermeable materials, such as cling film, to avoid condensation and mould growth. Wrapping also slows down the cooling process.

Blast chillers

This is equipment designed specifically for the rapid chilling of food. Usually, chilled air at 2°C to 7°C is circulated in a cabinet around the product. Some blast chillers use the vapour from liquid nitrogen and solid carbon dioxide. Some equipment can be set to hold foods after chilling, acting as a normal refrigerator. Alternatively, if suitable blast-chilling

Food must be cooled quickly

SUPERVISING FOOD SAFETY (LEVEL 3) The storage and temperature control of food

equipment is not available, hot food can be cooled rapidly in an otherwise empty freezer and taken out when safe temperatures have been reached, for storage in a refrigerator.

For cooling liquids, ice cream freezers can be used and, for very large quantities, vacuum chillers are available.

Food preparation

The main hazards likely to occur during preparation are cross-contamination, the multiplication of bacteria and the formation of toxins due to food being left at ambient temperatures for too long. The observance of good hygiene practices during food preparation is an essential element in preventing food poisoning. Raw food and high-risk food should be prepared in different areas with separate, clean equipment. Raw vegetables should be washed thoroughly in a separate sink, which is not used for washing utensils etc. and is positioned to avoid cross-contamination of high-risk food or clean utensils/equipment. Disposable wiping cloths should be used.

The handling of food should be minimized and food must not be left in a warm, humid atmosphere. The minimum amount of food should be prepared and then returned to refrigeration. Many schools and hospitals prepare food just prior to consumption, as required, as an additional safeguard. Food handlers should work in a logical, planned manner ensuring that working surfaces are kept as tidy as possible. Spillages and waste food should be cleared away promptly. Once again, staff training is essential.

The use of colour-coded utensils and chopping boards, e.g. red for raw food, will cut down the risk of cross-contamination. Only drinking water should be used in food preparation activities. Any ice in contact with food should be made from drinking water to prevent risk of contamination.

Food service

Care must be taken to prevent the contamination of food during service. High standards of personal hygiene and the implementation of good hygiene practices are essential. Food equipment and food-contact surfaces must be cleaned and disinfected. The handling of food should be minimized; tongs and serving utensils are preferred. Separate displays and separate staff should, if possible, be used by retail outlets serving both raw and high-risk food. If gloves are used these should be food grade and the hands should be washed before putting on the gloves and after taking them off. Gloves should be changed regularly and damaged gloves should be replaced immediately. Blue gloves are preferred in case a piece of damaged glove ends up in the food. Gloves can be contaminated just the same as hands.

Food on display must be protected from customers, e.g. with sneeze guards. Food should be maintained at or above 63ºC if hot and at or below 5ºC if cold. Food displays at ambient should be kept no longer than 2 hours if hot or 4 hours if cold.

Food served should be in good condition and within its shelf life. Ice-cream scoops should be kept clean, preferably in running water and not stored in a disinfectant solution which is quickly deactivated by ice cream.

SUPERVISING FOOD SAFETY (LEVEL 3) The storage and temperature control of food

If vending machines are used they must be kept clean and at the correct temperature (below 5ºC for high-risk food and –18ºC for frozen food). All stock should be subject to stock rotation.

Distribution of high-risk food

Vehicles used for the distribution of high-risk food must always be insulated and preferably refrigerated, even for short journeys. Insulation of the roof and floor is just as important as the insulation of the walls. Properly located thermometers should be fitted to all vehicles.

Vehicles must be maintained in a clean and tidy condition. Raw food should never be transported with high-risk food unless they are completely segregated to avoid any risk of contamination. Stacking of vehicles should facilitate sufficient air circulation around the food.

THE STORAGE OF FROZEN FOOD

At temperatures of around -40°C, most frozen food should keep for several years without noticeable deterioration. However, most catering and retail freezers operate at -18°C. At this temperature a gradual loss of flavour and a toughening of texture occurs. Above -10°C spoilage organisms commence growth and, together with enzymes, can cause serious problems including souring, putrefaction and rancidity.

All frozen food should be labelled and coded to enable traceability and recall in the event of problems.

Storage of frozen food at retail premises

To ensure that customers receive the highest quality of frozen food, managers must:

- only use reputable suppliers;
- reject deliveries above -15°C or which show signs of thawing or having been refrozen, for example, packs of peas which have welded solid;
- not allow frozen food to remain at ambient temperatures for longer than 15 minutes. Food will, of necessity, be at ambient temperatures during unloading of deliveries and stocking display units from back-up stores;
- not use display freezers for freezing fresh food, as they are only capable of maintaining the temperature of food which is already frozen;
- ensure that display units are not filled above the load line as this would result in thawing and deterioration;
- carry out regular inspections of freezers and check temperatures at least daily but preferably more frequently. Electronic probe thermometers, between the packs, should be used to ensure the accuracy of the indicating thermometers which should be fitted to all units in an easily readable position;
- ensure that back-up stores are fitted with strip-curtains or air blowers and the doors are opened as little as possible to avoid unacceptable fluctuations of temperature. Ice build-up on the walls or floor of units must not be allowed;

- implement effective systems of stock control and stock rotation. It is advisable to code food on delivery to assist rotation;
- all food must be suitably wrapped in moisture-impermeable film to prevent drying out of the surface (freezer burn);
- separate freezers should be used for raw and high-risk food; and
- ensure that food is not mishandled. Damage to packaging may result in loss of product, contamination and freezer burn.

Storage times

All food should be used within the time recommended by the manufacturer. However, a general guide for food kept at -18°C is:
- vegetables, fruit and most meat up to 12 months; and
- pork sausages, offal, fatty fish, butter and soft cheeses up to 6 months.

Salad vegetables, non-homogenized milk, single cream, eggs and bananas should not be frozen. Cream can be whipped and stabilized to overcome the separation in desserts. The star marking system is used to indicate the temperature and storage times of food in a frozen storage compartment. A four star freezer is capable of freezing food without affecting the food already in frozen storage.

Freezing and refreezing

Freezing of food will not improve its quality. The slow freezing of food in domestic freezers results in the formation of large ice crystals which rupture cells, leading to a slight deterioration in quality, due to changes in the composition of proteins in the presence of enzymes. This deterioration is much more noticeable if food is thawed and refrozen, apart from the obvious dangers if the thawed food is maintained above 10°C for a considerable time. Large ice crystals are particularly noticeable in ice cream which has been refrozen. However, food which has been frozen, thawed and thoroughly cooked may be refrozen quite safely, although flavour and texture will be altered and nutritional value lowered.

Effect of fluctuating temperatures

Clear plastic packaging of food may act as a greenhouse and the radiant heat from fluorescent tubes and air conditioning may increase the temperature of frozen food significantly. Fluctuations from 3°C to 18°C have been observed with the lower temperatures only being achieved during the night when heat sources have been switched off.

Freezer breakdown

If the freezer breaks down or food becomes thawed, for example, due to a power failure, the food may occasionally be treated as fresh. In certain circumstances the food may be cooked and refrozen. If the food has a solid core of ice it may be safe to refreeze without cooking. If in doubt advice should be obtained from the local Environmental Health Department.

In the event of breakdown, the lid of the freezer should be left closed and the unit covered in newspapers and blankets until repaired. Food may remain frozen for at least two days in a well-stocked, well-insulated freezer.

Thawing of frozen food

Many foods taken from the freezer can be cooked immediately but poultry, joints of meat and other large items must be completely thawed before cooking. The manufacturer's instructions should always be followed. If food is not completely thawed, ice is likely to be present at the centre and the heat from subsequent cooking will be used to melt the ice and not to raise the internal temperature above that required to destroy pathogens. In these situations the traditional cooking time should be extended and it is essential to check that a core temperature of 75°C has been achieved.

Thawing at room temperatures (25°C to 30°C) may result in the multiplication of bacteria on the warm surface of food, whilst the centre remains frozen. If food is thawed in a refrigerator it must be separated from other food and adequate time allowed to thaw completely. A 10kg turkey will take several days to thaw and the surfaces of the refrigerator, and high-risk food, may become contaminated with thawed liquid containing pathogenic bacteria. Thawing of frozen poultry is best carried out in a thawing cabinet or at 10°C to 15°C in a well-ventilated area entirely separate from other foods. Cold running water may be used but care must be taken to avoid contamination of the sink and surrounding surfaces. Thawed food which is not required for immediate use, should be marked with a new date code and stored under refrigeration.

Rules for handling frozen poultry

- segregate from high-risk food;
- thaw completely in a cool room at less than 15°C or in a thawing cabinet. Clean, cold running water is preferable to thawing in warm kitchen temperatures or in refrigerators with limited space. Poultry will be ready for cooking when the body is pliable, the legs are flexible and the body cavity is free from ice crystals;
- remove giblets;
- once thawed keep in the refrigerator, separate from high-risk food, and cook within 24 hours;
- cook thoroughly and cook the stuffing separately;
- all utensils and surfaces used for the preparation of raw meat and poultry should be thoroughly cleaned and disinfected before being used for high-risk food. It is preferable to use separate work surfaces;
- eat straight after cooking or maintain above 63°C or, if the bird is carved cold, cool it quickly and store in the refrigerator. As with all meats refrigerated storage is essential within 1.5 hours; and
- avoid handling the cooked bird unnecessarily.

COOK-CHILL

Cook-chill is the name given to a catering system in which food is thoroughly cooked and then chilled rapidly in a blast chiller to a temperature of 3°C or below within 1.5 hours. The food is stored between 0°C and 3°C until required for reheating. The food is usually produced in a central production unit (CPU) and transported to satellite kitchens for regeneration (reheating).

There are usually nine stages in a cook-chill system:

- bulk storage;
- cooking to at least 75°C;
- blast chilling;
- distribution at or below 3°C;
- serving.
- preparation;
- portioning, packaging and labelling;
- storage at or below 3°C;
- regeneration to at least 75°C; and

The following benefits are claimed for the cook-chill system:

- cost-effectiveness – fewer staff, reduction in overtime, shift and weekend working, central purchasing, better utilization of equipment and reduced floor space;
- better staff conditions and less work in unsociable hours. Staff turnover is usually reduced;
- flexibility – orders for meals can be accepted at much shorter notice;
- more accurate portioning and less wastage; and
- improved consistency, quality and palatability compared with meals kept hot, above 63°C, for long periods. Complaints of dried-up and overcooked food should not occur.

Cook-chill demands considerable management and supervisory skills and considerable forward planning. In order to ensure the safety of cook-chill the following rules should be observed:

- good quality raw materials;
- good design to ensure continuous workflow from raw material to finished product. Cross-contamination must be avoided;
- controlled thawing of frozen ingredients;
- the implementation of HACCP or systems based on the principles of HACCP;
- high standards of hygiene, especially personal hygiene;
- food cooked, without delay, to a minimum temperature of 75°C;
- food portioned and chilled to below 3°C within two hours of cooking;
- hygienic food containers utilized and date marked;
- the refrigerated store should maintain food at between 0°C to 3°C and should be fitted with indicating thermometers and alarms;
- the maximum life of the food is five days, including the day of production and the day of consumption;
- should the temperature of the food exceed 5°C it should be eaten within 12 hours; if the temperature exceeds 10°C during storage or distribution it should be destroyed;

- refrigerated vehicles are preferred for distribution but pre-chilled insulated containers may suffice for short journeys;
- food must be regenerated as soon as possible when removed from storage; and
- a centre temperature of at least 75°C should be achieved using effective heating units. Service should commence within 15 minutes and temperatures should not drop below 63°C.

Sous vide

Sous vide is a system of cooking raw or par-cooked food in a sealed pouch under vacuum. Core temperatures as high as 95°C for 2 minutes, or equivalent are required. The food should be blast chilled to below 3°C within 2 hours of cooking. In the UK a storage life of 8 days, including the day of production and consumption is the maximum recommended. The main risk is from anaerobic, spore-forming bacteria such as *Clostridium botulinum*. Spores will survive cooking and temperature abuse during storage may enable germination of spores and multiplication of vegetative bacteria.

COOK-FREEZE

The first four stages of cook-freeze are the same as cook-chill, namely bulk storage, preparation, cooking and portioning, packaging and labelling. The fifth stage is blast-freezing. Pre-cooked, lidded packs are loaded onto trolleys which are wheeled into tunnel-type blast-freezers which reduce the temperature to -20°C in less than 90 minutes. Rapid freezing is essential to avoid the formation of large ice crystals which result in poor texture and loss of nutritional value on regeneration. The frozen containers are kept at -20°C and may be stored for up to 12 months.

The exact number of meals required can be removed from storage on demand and regenerated to a temperature of at least 75°C in serving kitchens using, for example, forced-air convection ovens.

REHEATING AND HOT HOLDING

Reheating food presents a major potential hazard as food passes through the danger zone on three occasions. Bacterial growth may occur during the heating-up phase, the cooling phase and during any subsequent storage, if sufficiently high temperatures are not reached and then maintained. Generally, food should be reheated as rapidly as possible, to a temperature of at least 75°C (82°C in Scotland) and then held at 63°C or above, until served.

To ensure adequate reheating, bulk should be minimized and, to ensure rapid penetration of heat, 'surround' systems, such as specialist regeneration ovens, may be used. Microwave ovens are a successful and efficient means of reheating, providing the food has a high water content. However, domestic models should not be used in commercial practice. Commercial convector-microwave ovens are particularly useful.

Liquid products, such as soups, should be brought to the boil and kept boiling for several minutes before use, to ensure destruction of toxins. The hot liquids may then

SUPERVISING FOOD SAFETY (LEVEL 3) The storage and temperature control of food

need cooling before they can be served, to avoid scalding.

Hot holding

A variety of equipment is available for keeping food hot, pending service. Liquids, semi-liquids and particulate products, such as vegetables and ready-to-eat portions of meat, may be kept in *bains-marie*. These should always be brought up to operating temperature before use, and should not on any account be used for reheating foods. In water baths, checks should be made to ensure that the water levels are kept high. Topping-up should be with hot or boiling water. Container sizes should be matched to the water depth, limiting the amount of product which is above the water level.

Thorough reheating of food is essential

Hot cupboards and hot plates may be used for storing reheated products. The latter are particularly valuable when used in conjunction with heating light arrays, but care should be taken to ensure that foods are kept fully in the lit areas, which corresponds with the areas exposed to the radiant heat.

Hot food should be stored at or above 63ºC. The temperature of the food should be monitored at two hourly intervals using a clean disinfected probe thermometer. If food is below 63ºC it may be reheated, on one occasion, and stored above 63ºC or consumed. If hot food has been below 63ºC for longer than 2 hours it should be discarded.

Key points

- Raw food is likely to be contaminated with pathogenic micro-organisms and should be considered as potentially hazardous.
- Raw food should always be stored and prepared separate from ready-to-eat food.
- Vacuum packs should be stored under refrigeration.
- Satisfactory stock rotation is essential to avoid spoilage and waste food. Food must not be sold after its 'use-by' date.
- Refrigerators should usually operate between 1˚C and 4˚C.
- A core temperature of 75˚C is recommended for cooking most foods.
- Hot food must be cooled rapidly. Although joints may take up to eight hours to cool to 3˚C.
- Freezers should operate at -18˚C.
- Frozen poultry and large joints must be completely thawed prior to cooking.
- If food is stored hot it should be kept above 63˚C.
- If food is reheated a temperature of at least 75˚C, and 82˚C in Scotland, is required.
- Dry goods stores should be dry, cool and pest free.

7 Food spoilage and preservation

Immediately vegetables and fruit are harvested, fish are taken from the sea or animals are slaughtered, they start decomposing (spoiling). There are two ways in which this can occur:
- by the action of natural chemicals (enzymes) already in the food. These are known as autolytic (or self-splitting) enzymes; and
- by the action of enzymes from bacteria, moulds and yeasts. These are released by the organisms to break down the food so that it can be absorbed by them.

Spoilage usually starts with aerobes and facultative anaerobes. Then, as the oxygen is used up, obligate anaerobes take over. Moulds and yeasts tend to cause spoilage when the conditions do not favour bacterial growth. Signs of spoilage include discolouration, off odours and taste, slime, rancidity, gas production and changes to the taste and texture. Cans and packs may 'blow'.

How quickly food spoils depends on the condition of the food, the pH, water availability, temperature, oxygen, the presence of inhibitory substances (preservatives) and the type and number of spoilage organisms present.

Insects or vermin, and parasites, can also spoil food. So can some chemicals which, even at very low levels, can cause unacceptable taint. Contamination, and the action of oxygen (oxidation), can cause deterioration. Even excessive cold can cause damage by extracting water from the food, a fault known as freezer burn.

Foods which are most prone to spoilage are known as 'perishable'. These include meat, poultry, fish, dairy products, fruit and vegetables. Foods such as sugar, flour and dried fruit, are unlikely to be affected by spoilage unless they are handled badly, for example, by storing under damp conditions. These are often described as stable or 'non-perishable'.

The presence of mould usually results in food having a musty odour and flavour and, although usually considered harmless, increasing concern is being expressed about fungal toxins known as mycotoxins.

The acidity of fruit ensures that most primary spoilage is caused by moulds and yeasts which are able to multiply at higher acidity than bacteria. Thus, vegetables stored in vinegar, such as beetroot, may be attacked by yeasts. Yeast spoilage of food can often be detected by the alcoholic taste and smell and the presence of bubbles in liquid. Moulds are responsible for most of the spoilage of baked products, especially bread and pies. As mould spores are destroyed by normal cooking temperatures, the spoilage usually arises from airborne spores and contact with contaminated surfaces after cooking.

Rope in bread and other bakery products is caused by a spore-forming bacterium in the flour. Affected bread becomes yellow or brown and develops a fruity, sickly smell and a soft sticky texture. Chemical preservatives are used to prevent rope.

Staleness of bread usually develops with prolonged holding, due to physical changes in the carbohydrates. Refrigeration increases the rate of staling; however, staling does not occur during frozen storage at -18°C.

Rancidity

Rancidity is the term used to describe the breakdown of fats or fatty substances. It occurs when the fats are broken down into free fatty acids by naturally occurring enzymes, known as lipases. These can also be produced by micro-organisms. Heating may destroy lipase-producing bacteria but not any lipase already formed and rancidity may still occur.

Rancidity may also occur as a result of the interaction between fats and oxygen, often in the presence of copper or iron contamination. The prolonged cold storage of fatty fish, bacon and pork results in rancidity unless vacuum packed.

FOOD PRESERVATION

Preservation is the treatment of food to prevent or delay spoilage and inhibit growth of pathogenic organisms which would render the food unfit. Preservation may involve:
- the use of low temperatures or high temperatures;
- moisture reduction;
- the use of chemicals;
- acid fermentation;
- controlled atmospheres and the restriction of oxygen (vacuum packing);
- smoking; and
- irradiation.

Food preservation: smoking

Food preservation by the use of low temperatures

This form of preservation is primarily to prevent spoilage by micro-organisms, the enzyme-producing activity of which is slowed down or arrested by low temperatures. Temperatures used may be:
- above freezing (refrigerator);
- below freezing (freezer); and
- at freezing (commercially used with chilled beef).

Temperatures above freezing

Refrigerators, operating at between 1°C and 4°C, are suitable for the short-term storage of most perishable foods. Most common pathogenic organisms stop growing below 5°C. Some can continue to grow down to about -2°C, although the growth rate is slow. Certain spoilage bacteria, and moulds, can also cause spoilage at refrigeration temperatures.

Temperatures below freezing

Freezing reduces the moisture available for bacterial growth and significantly reduces enzyme activity. It also destroys some bacteria, including pathogens, and a gradual reduction occurs during storage. Some parasites can also be destroyed by freezing. However, bacterial spores and toxins are generally unaffected.

Moulds and yeasts are more likely to grow on frozen food than bacteria as they are better able to withstand the reduced water availability and the low temperatures. In practice very few organisms grow below -10°C. On thawing, however, surviving bacteria can grow rapidly, compensating for those destroyed, especially if food reaches temperatures of 20°C or higher.

Before vegetables are frozen they must be blanched by dipping in hot water for a short period, approximately one minute. Blanching destroys enzymes which produce off-odours and flavours, and reduces the bacterial load. It also fixes colour, removes trapped air and softens some vegetables, which helps packing. Overblanching will result in excessive loss of vitamin C.

During the freezing process, ice crystals are formed. The slower the rate of freezing, the larger are the ice crystals formed, which can damage certain foods. To avoid this, quick freezing techniques are used.

Most foods will keep for prolonged periods in a freezer, although a recommended shelf life is given because of loss of texture, flavour, tenderness, colour and overall nutritional quality.

Foods must be properly wrapped to avoid loss of moisture from the surface, i.e. freezer burn. The oxidation of food is slower at -18°C and this also assists in preservation. However, vacuum packing is essential to extend the shelf life of frozen food susceptible to oxidative rancidity, for example, bacon.

Freezing systems

There are several commercial systems used to freeze food. Air-blast freezing is the commonest. It uses static tunnels where trolleys of boxed product, such as beef and cakes, are passed through. Solid continuous-belt freezers are used for fish fillets, patties and pizzas. Air circulates around the food at temperatures of -30°C to -40°C. Plate freezing is used for food packed in flat cartons, for example, fish blocks and ready-meals. The cartons are placed between narrow metal shelves in which a very cold refrigerant circulates, so ensuring freezing. For products like peas, a process called fluidized-bed freezing can be used. The food is moved along a tunnel on a perforated tray, borne along by a cushion of freezing air forced up from below. Each item is individually quick frozen. In cryogenic freezing, food is sprayed with, or dipped into, a refrigerant such as liquid nitrogen. This is very quick, although more expensive than conventional techniques.

FOOD PRESERVATION BY THE USE OF HIGH TEMPERATURES

Heat treatment is used to destroy enzymes and spoilage and pathogenic organisms and so preserve food. However, heat-resistant bacteria, some toxins and spores may survive. Furthermore, unless very high time/temperature combinations are used, some normal bacteria will survive. The number depends on the initial loading, the strain of organism, the acidity and the presence of protective substances such as proteins and fats.

To prevent recontamination of food after processing, suitable packaging is used, for example, bottles or cans, which can also prevent the multiplication of surviving bacteria. Alternatively, or additionally, products are kept refrigerated.

Pasteurization

Pasteurization involves heating food at a relatively low temperature for a short time, sufficient to kill target pathogens while keeping changes to the food at a minimum. A slight reduction in vitamins and nutritional value will occur. The process is commonly applied to milk, which may be heated at 72°C for 15 seconds and immediately cooled to below 10°C. The actual time and temperature combination chosen depends on the type of food and must be sufficient to destroy vegetative pathogens and most spoilage organisms, although *Lacto bacillus* can survive. Liquid egg can be pasteurized at 64.4°C for at least 2.5 minutes. Following pasteurization, the treated egg must satisfy the alpha-amylase test. Toxins and spores generally survive pasteurization. Pasteurized products spoil more quickly than most other forms of heat treated products.

Sterilization

Sterilization involves the destruction of all micro-organisms. This is sometimes difficult to achieve, so processes are often designed only to destroy viable organisms, i.e. not spores. In this case food is considered 'commercially sterile'. This means that organisms surviving treatment will be of no significance under normal methods of storage. Low-acid canned food is given such a treatment. Sterilization temperatures normally exceed 100°C and are usually achieved by means of steam under pressure.

The main advantage of sterilization is prolonged shelf life. The main objections are a lowering of nutritional value, including loss of vitamins, and a marked difference in texture and flavour.

Ultra heat treatment (UHT)

The ultra heat treatment of milk is a technique used to extend its shelf life without the changes caused by sterilization. Nutritional value is similar to that of pasteurized milk. Milk is heated to a temperature of not less than 135°C for one second before filling aseptically into sterile containers. This reduces the amount of caramelization and also enhances keeping quality. UHT milk will keep for several months without refrigeration.

Cooking

Cooking is a form of preservation but is essentially used to make food more palatable and safe for immediate consumption. Temperatures achieved during cooking are usually sufficient to ensure an effective reduction, or the elimination, of vegetative pathogens, although some preformed toxins and spores may be unaffected. In some cases, cooking activates spores and a significant multiplication of vegetative bacteria may occur during subsequent cooling. Internal temperatures of at least 75°C should be achieved to ensure bacteriological safety, although heating food to a lower temperature for longer periods of time may be equally as effective.

Cooked products, such as vegetables, will deteriorate more rapidly than raw products, and other methods of preservation must be used to prolong shelf life if stored, for example, refrigeration, freezing or canning.

Canning

Unlike most other forms of preservation the food inside the can remains an ideal medium for bacterial growth. It is therefore imperative that:
- the heat process destroys all anaerobic pathogenic and spoilage micro-organisms;
- the closure of the can precludes the entry of micro-organisms; and
- the post-process handling of the can prevents damage and subsequent contamination.

The most heat-resistant pathogenic organism is *Clostridium botulinum* and this bacterium will not grow below a pH of 4.5. Consequently, when determining the heat process, regard must be had for the pH of the can contents. All foods with a pH of less than 4.5 are known as acid foods and those with a pH of more than 4.5 are termed low-acid foods.

Most fruits have a pH of less than 4.5 and consequently only receive a relatively low pasteurizing heat process. Vegetables and meats have pHs much higher than 4.5 and they are given a process known as a 'botulinum cook' to render them commercially sterile.

Before canned food is heat processed it is normally prepared in some way. The actual process of preparation will vary depending on the food type but the following flow chart shows the usual processes involved.

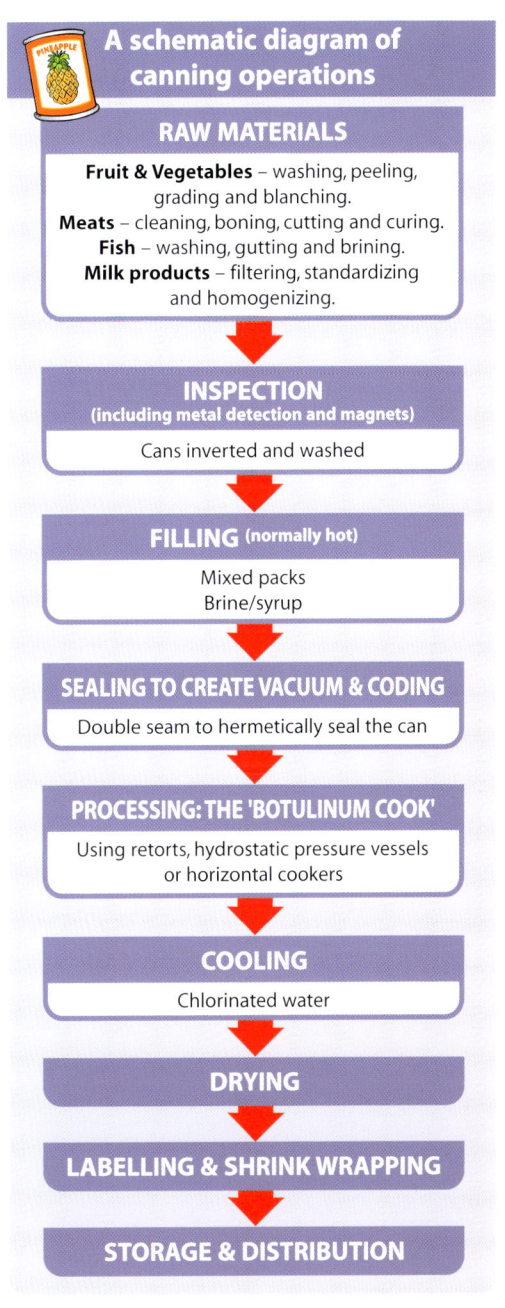

A schematic diagram of canning operations

RAW MATERIALS
Fruit & Vegetables – washing, peeling, grading and blanching.
Meats – cleaning, boning, cutting and curing.
Fish – washing, gutting and brining.
Milk products – filtering, standardizing and homogenizing.

INSPECTION (including metal detection and magnets)
Cans inverted and washed

FILLING (normally hot)
Mixed packs
Brine/syrup

SEALING TO CREATE VACUUM & CODING
Double seam to hermetically seal the can

PROCESSING: THE 'BOTULINUM COOK'
Using retorts, hydrostatic pressure vessels or horizontal cookers

COOLING
Chlorinated water

DRYING

LABELLING & SHRINK WRAPPING

STORAGE & DISTRIBUTION

The minimum safe thermal process for a low-acid canned food is one which would reduce the chance of survival of one spore of *Clostridium botulinum* to less than one in 10^{12}. This is achieved by ensuring the core of the food reaches a minimum of 121°C for three minutes, or an equivalent time and temperature combination. After the heating process the cans must be cooled with chlorinated water. The greatest care must be taken after heat treatment, especially whilst the can is still warm and wet, and before the sealing compound has hardened. Bacteria are capable of being sucked into visually satisfactory cans through microscopic holes in the seams. If these bacteria are spoilage or pathogenic organisms, problems will occur. Warm, wet cans must not be handled.

Pasteurized canned foods

As discussed earlier, most low-acid canned foods are processed to a minimum standard of the 'botulinum cook'. However, some foods if fully processed would be inedible. One example of this is canned cured ham. This product only receives a pasteurization process (a centre temperature of about 70°C). This means that chilled storage is essential to ensure its safety.

DEHYDRATION AS A MEANS OF PRESERVATION

All micro-organisms need moisture to multiply. Dehydration reduces the amount of available water and thus prevents growth. However, some bacterial spores will germinate on the reconstitution of the dried product. Although yeasts and moulds usually grow at lower moisture levels than do bacteria, mould spoilage is also prevented, as is enzyme activity. Provided dried foods are stored in suitable airtight packs, and kept dry, they will keep for a considerable period of time.

Sun drying was the earliest method of dehydration and is still practised in hot climates, for example, for drying currants, raisins and figs. Artificial drying is quicker and normally more effective than natural means. Unfortunately, food undergoes irreversible changes to the tissue structure during drying, which affects both texture and flavour.

Artificial drying techniques include the use of hot air, for example in tunnel drying, fluidized-bed drying, roller drying and spray drying. Changes in protein structure and flavour can be reduced by using warm air, as in accelerated freeze drying. The choice of technique often depends on the type of foodstuff and the degree of dehydration required. Blanching of vegetables must be carried out before drying to obviate enzyme activity during storage.

In spray drying, a solution, paste or slurry is dispersed as small droplets into a stream of hot air. The small droplets result in a rapid loss of moisture and a large proportion of the colour, flavour and nutritive value of the food is maintained. However, because the evaporative cooling effect keeps the temperature of the droplets low, a pasteurization process is usually required prior to spray drying.

In roller drying, the food is turned into a paste which is dried on a heated drum and scraped off. Generally, product quality is inferior to spray-dried product. For fruits and vegetables, a tunnel drier, 10 to 15 metres long, is used. Trays of product are passed through it while hot air is blown across the trays. This continuous process leads to a gradual loss of moisture. Total removal of moisture may not be necessary. The remaining water forms a strong solution with salts and soluble proteins. This water remaining is not available to micro-organisms.

Accelerated freeze drying
Food is frozen quickly and then lightly heated under vacuum. Ice in the food is then extracted as water vapour, a process known as sublimation. The process minimizes the effects of drying and the product reconstitutes better.

CHEMICAL METHODS OF PRESERVATION

A wide range of chemical additives is available for food preservation and may be used to prevent microbial spoilage, chemical deterioration and mould growth. As high concentration of some chemicals, such as sulphur dioxide and sodium nitrate are poisonous, the use of additives is strictly controlled by legislation and maximum permitted levels are usually specified. Preservatives used include:

(1) Salt: Salt reduces the water available (a_W) to bacteria. Its effectiveness depends on the concentration, contamination levels, pH, temperature, protein content and the presence of other inhibitory substances. In use, it may be rubbed into meat or, as brine, injected into the muscular tissue. It can also be an ingredient in the manufacture of sausages and used to preserve fish.

Some micro-organisms are salt-tolerant but this tolerance is usually decreased by lowering the temperature or the pH. Moulds are less affected by salt. Staphylococci will grow in relatively high salt concentrations and are often associated with food poisoning from semi-preserved salted meats.

In preservation the use of salt, with the addition of other chemicals such as sodium nitrate, is termed curing. Its use for flavour or colouring is termed brining.

(2) Nitrates and nitrites: Sodium nitrate and sodium nitrite salts are used in curing meat. They help retain colour and reduce spoilage. They are also essential in such products as pasteurized ham to stop the production of botulinum toxin, by preventing the germination of spores.

Traditionally, salt and nitrate solutions were injected into meat, which was then immersed in brine to enable salt tolerant bacteria to convert nitrate to nitrite. Currently, nitrites tend to be used direct as they are much more effective than nitrates.

The effectiveness of curing salts depends on various factors, including the pH of the meat, the number and types of micro-organisms present and the curing temperature.

(3) Sugar: Sugar acts in a similar manner to salt but concentrations need to be about six times higher. It is commonly used for jam and other preserves, candied fruit and condensed milk. Certain types of cake have increased shelf life due to the effect of sugar.

(4) Sulphur dioxide/sulphite: Sulphur dioxide may be used in gaseous or liquid form or as a salt. It is an antioxidant and also inhibits growth of bacteria and moulds. It is used in some foods to prevent enzymatic browning. Sulphur dioxide is also used in wine, beers, fruit juice and comminuted meat products, including sausages, where it is allowed up to 450μg/g. Apart from reducing the growth of spoilage organisms, sulphur dioxide also limits the growth of salmonellae.

(5) Pickling/acidification: This process involves using an acid such as acetic acid, i.e. vinegar, to acidify the food to create an environment in which micro-organisms will not multiply. The acidification process is controlled so that the pH of each part of the product drops below 4.5.

(6) Sodium and calcium propionate: Propionates are active in low-acid foods and very useful to prohibit mould growth. They are used in bread, cakes, cheese, grain and jellies.

(7) Antibiotics: These chemicals have a preservative role in addition to their normal function. Their use is strictly controlled by regulations to avoid the build-up of resistance by pathogenic organisms. An example of an antibiotic used for preservation is nisin, added to some cheeses and canned foods. Nisin is heat-resistant but is destroyed during digestion and should not cause problems of pathogen drug resistance.

FERMENTATION

Fermented foods are produced by the activities of bacteria, yeasts or moulds and include cheese, yoghurt, salami, sauerkraut, pepperoni, bread and soy sauce. The fermentation process involves the use of starter cultures, for example lactic acid bacteria added to milk to produce yoghurt. Lactic acid bacteria ferment carbohydrates such as glucose to produce lactic acid which lowers the pH to preserve the food. Yeast fermentation produces carbon dioxide and ethanol.

CONTROLLED ATMOSPHERES

One of the simplest food preservation methods is to change the atmosphere around the food. This is termed modified atmosphere packaging (MAP). The proportion of the gases normally present around a product is modified to contain, for example, lower levels of oxygen and higher levels of nitrogen and carbon dioxide. This slows down the growth of many spoilage organisms and extends shelf life. MAP should also be combined with correct chilled temperature control in order to guarantee the control of microbial proliferation.

The restriction of oxygen

The development of oxidative rancidity and the growth of strict aerobes such as moulds can be prevented by vacuum packing, although sufficient oxygen normally remains in vacuum packs of meat to facilitate the growth of some aerobes. Complete removal of oxygen allows the growth of anaerobes such as *Clostridium perfringens*.

Vacuum packs of cooked meat must be stored under refrigeration to achieve a reasonable shelf life.

SMOKING

Smoking is applied primarily to meat and fish, after brining or pickling, by suspending the food over smouldering hardwoods such as oak and ash. It is often used only to enhance flavour. Smoking also has some dehydrating effect and there may be some preserving action due to the presence of bactericidal chemicals in smoke. Most non-sporing bacteria will be destroyed but moulds and *Cl. botulinum* type E may survive, especially in low salt concentrations. Smoked products should, therefore, be refrigerated at 3°C or below.

Cold smoked food should be treated as raw and hot smoked food should be considered as high-risk food.

Another way of adding a smoke flavour to the food is to spray a liquid, produced by trapping smoke in water, on to the food. The preserving effect is limited and the food is not dehydrated.

FOOD IRRADIATION

This form of preservation involves subjecting the food to a dose of ionizing radiation. It is an effective and safe method of extending shelf life. It destroys parasites, insects including eggs, bacteria, moulds and yeasts. However, microbial spores and toxins remain unaffected at the levels used. Foods most commonly irradiated outside the UK include chicken, fish, prawns, onions, potatoes, spices and strawberries. Irradiation may be used as part of a continuous or batch process. (In the UK only spices may be subject to irradiation.)

Preservation using irradiation has the same limitations as many other preservation techniques. Vitamins may be destroyed and enzymes are not deactivated. Other disadvantages include the encouragement of oxidative rancidity in fatty foods, the possible production of free radicals in food that stimulate a range of chemical reactions, and the softening of some fruit.

Key points

- Spoilage of food commences when vegetables and fruit are harvested, animals are slaughtered and fish are removed from the sea.
- Spoilage occurs because of the action of enzymes, bacteria, moulds, yeasts and pests.
- Refrigeration of perishable foods slows down spoilage.
- Food preservation prevents or delays spoilage and inhibits the growth of pathogenic organisms.
- Preservation may involve: the use of low or high temperatures; dehydration; chemicals; controlled atmospheres and physical methods.
- Foods should be cooked to a centre temperature of at least 75°C.

8 The design and construction of food premises and equipment

A well-planned layout and the use of satisfactory building materials are essential to achieve high standards of hygiene. The size of the premises must facilitate efficient operation and the site must be large enough to accommodate possible future expansion.

Selection of a suitable site

The site must have sufficient services, i.e. electricity and gas, water supply and effluent disposal, and be accessible for delivery and waste disposal. It should not be liable to flooding or unacceptable contamination from chemicals, dust, odour or pests. Potential for noise emissions should be considered if there are nearby residential premises.

General principles of design

To achieve a satisfactory design, the following principles should be considered:

- clean and dirty processes must be separated to minimize the risk of contamination. Colour coding may be used. Where possible:
  a. work areas should be segregated into pre-cook and post-cook; and
  b. a separate area should be provided for de-boxing and unwrapping raw materials.
- workflow should be linear and progress in a uniform direction from raw material to finished product (from dirty to clean). This is essential to minimize risk of cross-contamination. Distances travelled by raw materials, utensils, food containers, waste food, packaging materials and staff should be minimized;
- facilities for personal hygiene and disinfection of small items of equipment should relate to working areas and process risks;
- where appropriate, suitable facilities must be provided for temperature, humidity and other controls;
- the premises must be capable of being thoroughly cleaned and, if necessary, disinfected at the end of production;
- insects, rodents and birds must be denied access and harbourage;
- yard surfaces and roads within the boundary of the premises must have a suitable impervious surface with adequate drainage, and provision made for refuse storage; and
- suitable provision must be made for staff welfare, including cloakroom and, if necessary, canteen and first-aid facilities.

THE CONSTRUCTION OF FOOD PREMISES

It is essential that the correct materials are chosen for all internal finishes and that they are properly fixed or applied. Materials should be non-toxic, durable and easy to maintain and clean.

Ceilings

Suspended ceilings are advantageous as horizontal pipework and services can be concealed in the ceiling void. They are normally constructed from a metal lattice incorporating cleansable panels. Aluminium backed and faced fibre-board has proved successful in many food factories. Flush-fitting ventilation grilles and lighting will often be provided.

Solid ceilings should be well insulated (to prevent condensation and mould growth), smooth, fire resistant, light-coloured, and coved at wall joints. Finishes should be washable. A non-flaking emulsion may be suitable. Special attention must be paid to ceiling finishes above heat and/or steam-producing appliances such as ovens, sinks and retorts. Canopies and separate extraction units may be fitted in these areas.

Ceiling height will vary depending on the type of operations being carried out but should be high enough to provide satisfactory working conditions and allow the installation of equipment.

Walls

Smooth, impervious, non-flaking, durable, light-coloured wall surfaces are required which must be capable of being thoroughly cleaned and, if necessary, disinfected. Dark coloured wall surfaces don't reflect light and dirt is more difficult to see. Internal solid walls are preferable to those with cavities.

When constructing factories, it can be advantageous to use modular buildings, of standard dimensions, with the actual production areas built inside the external structure, leaving clear walkways outside these areas, but within the overall structure. The 'building within the building' can be fabricated from modular panels of the type used for cold-store construction.

Wall surfaces in use include resin-bonded fibre glass, ceramic-faced blocks, plastic panelling, epoxy resin, glazed tiles with water-resistant grouting and rubberized paint on hard plaster or sealed brickwork. Some paints incorporate a fungicidal additive. Galvanized steel, aluminium and stainless steel are also used, and plastic sheeting is popular. Wall or floor stops are needed to prevent doors damaging wall surfaces, and wall corners should be protected. Crash rails should be used if trolleys are likely to damage wall surfaces, although large, angled fillets to the wall-floor junctions can also prevent trolley impact.

Pipework and ducting should be bracketed at least 150mm from walls to facilitate cleaning. All lagging to pipes must be smooth and impervious. Pipes passing through external walls must be effectively sealed to prevent the ingress of pests.

Windows and doors

Any windows should either be fixed on north-facing walls to reduce glare and solar heat gains, or treated with solar film to counteract heat gain. Openable windows are required to improve ventilation and reduce condensation. Cleansable, well-fitting fly-screens must, where necessary, be fitted to opening windows. Windows should be constructed to facilitate cleaning and any internal window sills should be sloped to prevent their use as shelves.

Doors should have smooth, non-absorbent surfaces capable of being thoroughly cleaned. They should be tight-fitting and self-closing. Door handles and finger-plates should be capable of disinfection. Swing doors with kick-plates are preferable to handles. External doorways should, where necessary, be proofed against the entry of insects, and metal kick-plates should be provided to prevent gnawing by rodents. Clear plastic strips can be used to protect openings.

Floors

Regard must be had to initial cost, durability, performance and safety. In food premises, floors should be durable, non-absorbent, anti-slip, without crevices and capable of being effectively cleaned. Where appropriate they must be resistant to acids, grease and salts and should slope sufficiently for liquids to drain to trapped gullies or channels; a slope (or 'fall') of 1 in 60 is the minimum recommended. The junctions between walls and floors should be coved.

Suitable flooring includes epoxy resin, granolithic (concrete incorporating granite chippings), welded anti-slip, vinyl sheet and slip-resistant ceramic or quarry tiles. Untreated concrete is unsuitable as it is porous, dusty and difficult to clean.

Cardboard or sawdust should not be placed on floor surfaces as it absorbs grease, moisture, bacteria and dirt. Sawdust can be blown onto food and cardboard causes a trip hazard.

Services

These include gas, electricity, water supplies, drainage, lighting and ventilation.

Gas supplies

Supply pipes should always be mounted clear of the floor and never so close to other pipes as to restrict access for cleaning. Flexible connections, to facilitate removal of equipment for cleaning purposes, are recommended.

Electrical supplies

Adequate numbers of power points should be available for all electrical equipment. Cut-out switches for power circuits should be accessible and separate from lighting and ventilation supplies, so that cleaning can take place in safety. Separate cut-out switches should be provided for refrigeration equipment.

Controls should be fixed clear of equipment to avoid becoming dirty or wet during cleaning. Removable electrical components assist cleaning and are advantageous. Surface-mounted electrical wiring should be protected by waterproof conduits. All switches should be flush-fitting and waterproof (especially in production areas).

Water supplies

Cold water supplies for use with food, for cleaning equipment or surfaces or for personal hygiene must be potable (of drinking water standard). They should not be fed via an intermediate tank unless chlorinated; mains supplies are preferable.

Water heating provisions should be able to supply hot water at a target discharge temperature of 60°C, although higher system temperatures may be required to avoid legionnaire's disease. In this case, mixer taps will be needed to avoid scalding. In hard-water areas, provision for softening should be made.

Non-potable water must be conveyed in identifiable systems which have no connection with, nor any possible reflux into, the potable water system. An external water supply should always be available.

Drainage

Premises should have an efficient, smooth-bore drainage system. Drains and sewers should be adequate to remove peak loads quickly without flooding. Sufficient drains should be installed to facilitate effective cleaning of rooms by pressure jet cleaners or other means. Channels or trapped gullies may be used. Grease traps, if fitted, should be large enough to allow adequate time for fat to separate and should be emptied regularly.

The direction of flow should be from clean areas to dirty areas. Toilets should feed into the system after food rooms. Inspection chambers should be placed outside food rooms but if interior location is unavoidable they must be airtight, i.e. triple seal, bolt down. All drainage systems must be provided with sufficient access points to allow rodding in the event of blockages. Petrol interceptors may be required for yard drains.

Drains should be constructed to inhibit the harbourage and movement of vermin. All external rainwater fall-pipes should be fitted with balloon guards to prevent rodent access. Circumference guards should be fitted around all vertical pipes fastened to walls, to prevent rodents climbing up them.

Ventilation

Sufficient ventilation must be provided to produce a satisfactory, safe working environment and to reduce humidities and temperatures which would encourage condensation and the rapid multiplication of bacteria. Condensation encourages mould growth and the multiplication of bacteria and drips onto food. Normally, ambient temperatures should be below 25°C. Natural ventilation often needs supplementing by mechanical ventilation to ensure effective air circulation and adequate air changes. You cannot rely on open windows. Extract ventilation should always flow from a clean to a dirty area. Its function is to prevent excessive heat build-up, condensation, dust, steam, and to remove odours and contaminated air. The source of input air must always be checked to ensure contaminants are not brought in to food rooms.

Steam-producing equipment, such as cookers, boilers and blanchers, should be provided with adequately-sized canopies. Provision of lower heat-emitting equipment such as pressure vessels and microwave ovens, and upgrading insulation on ovens will reduce heat production.

SUPERVISING FOOD SAFETY (LEVEL 3) The design and construction of food premises and equipment

Lighting

Suitable and sufficient lighting must be provided throughout food premises, including store rooms, passageways and stairways, so that employees can identify hazards and carry out tasks correctly.

Artificial lighting is often preferred to natural lighting because of problems of solar heat gain, glare, shadows and flying insects entering open windows. Recommended illumination levels are as follows: 150 lux in storerooms and 500 lux in preparation areas. Fluorescent tubes, fitted with diffusers to prevent glare and product contamination in the event of breakage, are recommended.

Handwashing facilities

Adequate facilities for handwashing and drying should be provided wherever the process demands. In particular, a suitable number of basins or troughs should be sited at the entrance of food rooms to ensure all persons entering wash their hands. Wash-hand basins must be easily accessible, should only be used for washing hands and should not be obstructed. All basins and

Inaccessible wash-hand basins

troughs, preferably made of stainless steel, should be connected to drains by properly trapped waste pipes. Wash-hand basins should be clean and provided with hot and cold water, liquid soap, drying facilities and a sign indicating that they are for handwashing only. They should not be used for any other purpose. A clean nailbrush may also be provided. Mixer taps are preferable so hands can be washed under warm running water. Non-hand operable infrared taps are preferred as they reduce the risk of cross-contamination.

Cleaning and disinfection facilities

Where appropriate, adequate facilities for the cleaning and disinfection of utensils, crockery, cutlery, glasses and equipment should be provided. These facilities will normally be constructed from stainless steel. Twin sinks are preferable to facilitate washing and disinfecting/rinsing. Sinks should be freestanding so that they can be removed easily after unscrewing the lower trap joint, freeing the waste pipe. 'Sterilizing' sinks and units should be capable of operating at 82°C.

Separate sinks must be provided for food preparation and equipment washing if the volume demands it. In small operations the same sink may be used if there is no risk to food safety. Exclusive food sinks may be provided with cold water only. Washing machines should not be sited in kitchens as this will involve bringing soiled and contaminated laundry into the kitchen. In the case of small nursing homes and guest houses this may even involve bedding and towels contaminated with body fluids. Laundry rooms should always be kept separate from kitchens to avoid the risk of contaminating food.

Sanitary conveniences and washing facilities

All new premises should be provided with adequate staff sanitary accommodation, adequately ventilated and lit. They should be kept clean and tidy. Rooms containing sanitary conveniences must be readily accessible but must not communicate directly with a room where food is processed, prepared or eaten. Internal wall and floor surfaces should permit wet cleaning.

Foot-operated flushing devices are recommended. Doors to intervening spaces and sanitary accommodation should be self-closing and clearly illustrate the sex of the user. Suitable and sufficient washing facilities must be provided at readily accessible places. In particular, facilities must be provided in the immediate vicinity of every sanitary convenience and supplied with clean, hot and cold or warm water, liquid soap and appropriate drying facilities.

Cloakrooms and lockers

Adequate accommodation for outdoor clothing and footwear, not worn by the staff during normal working hours, must be available. Such articles must not be stored in a food room unless in suitable cupboards or lockers provided only for this purpose. Adequate facilities for drying wet clothing should also be provided. Cloakrooms must be kept clean and tidy as scraps of food and other materials may attract cockroaches and rodents.

The storage and disposal of waste

Waste disposal systems must be planned, along with other services, when food premises are designed. Refuse collectors should not have to enter food rooms or dining areas.

Waste food should be kept separate from paper and cardboard packaging. In some instances, waste may be stored under refrigeration pending collection, for example, bones in butchers' shops. It is preferable for all waste food to be removed from food premises

Dustbins must be kept clean

at least daily and general refuse to be removed at least twice a week. Accumulations of refuse in food rooms are illegal, attract pests and encourage the multiplication of bacteria. They create odours, prevent effective cleaning and expose food to risk of microbiological and physical contamination. Suitable, impervious, easy-to-clean containers with foot-operated lids should be provided in food rooms. Disposable plastic sacks are also ideal. Regular emptying of internal waste bins is important, even if the bins are not full. This will reduce unpleasant odours, maintain adequate capacity and minimize bacterial multiplication and insect problems, for example, from maggots. Hazards that result from poor waste storage include:
- the attraction/multiplication of pests;
- the contamination of food (microbiological, chemical or physical); and
- the multiplication of bacteria.

Suitable facilities must be provided for the storage of waste externally, prior to removal from the establishment. Dustbins or bulk containers are commonly used, although skips and compactors are more appropriate for food factories. Compactors vary from units similar to a large dustbin to refuse-sack compactors and skip rams.

Dustbins should be stored clear of the ground, for example, on tubular steel racks, to facilitate cleaning and removal of spillages. All receptacles should be capable of being cleaned and provided with suitable tight-fitting lids or covers to prevent insects, birds and rodents gaining access. Overflowing bins attract pests.

The refuse area must have a well-drained, impervious surface which is capable of being kept clean. Standpipes, hoses and, possibly, high-pressure sprayers should be provided for cleaning purposes. Covered areas to protect refuse from the sun and rain are recommended. Satisfactory provision should be made for the disposal of liquid food waste such as oil.

Refuse areas should be secure and not be too far from food rooms to discourage their use but they should not be too close to encourage flies to enter the food rooms. They should not be sited next to the main food delivery entrance. Covered ways between refuse areas and food rooms are useful to protect staff against inclement weather.

Perimeter areas

It is recommended that a concrete path, at least 675mm wide, abutting the external walls should be provided around all food buildings. This removes cover for rodents and enables early signs of pests to be discovered, for example, rodent droppings. Paths should be kept clean, free of vegetation and inspected regularly. A smooth band of rendering, around 450mm, at the base of external walls will discourage rodents from climbing. Whenever possible, a perimeter fence should be constructed around food premises to deter unauthorized entry. Areas within perimeter fences must be kept clean and tidy. Rubbish, old equipment and weeds must not be allowed to accumulate or provide harbourage for insects or rodents.

Kitchen design

The layout of a well-designed commercial kitchen has three main characteristics:
- ♦ clearly identified and separated flows;
- ♦ defined accommodation, specific to the purposes allocated; and
- ♦ economy of space provision (commensurate with good hygiene practice).

The unit should also afford management personnel easy access to the areas under their control and good visibility in the areas which have to be supervised. Space is needed for management function and for equipment such as telephones and computers.

Flows

Four separate flows need to be considered: the food being produced; personnel; containers, utensils and equipment; and waste/refuse. Product flows should be subdivided into high-risk and contaminated (raw food) sections. Clear segregation should be maintained between the two. As far as practicable, flows should be unidirectional, without backtracking or crossover.

Accommodation

Accommodation should be sized according to operational need when at maximum production. Essentially, the working areas, stores, the equipment and its relative spacing should all be determined and laid out to suit the operation.

Areas should be allocated according to environmental compatibility; hot functions with hot, dirty with dirty, wet with wet, dry with dry, defined overall by segregation between high-risk and contaminated food handling.

Equipment required for specific functions should be grouped and accessible, in order to avoid excessive walking and the temptation to take shortcuts. Wash-hand basins should be strategically located to ensure that operatives entering food preparation areas wash their hands.

Size

There should be a minimum of circulation and dead space, commensurate with the efficient functioning of the unit. Size should be neither too small nor too large; there are penalties in the over-provision of space as much as there are problems with too small a provision.

The size of the kitchen can only be determined when its exact purpose and function have been defined. Items to take into consideration include:
- the state of raw materials, for example, ready prepared or not;
- the extent of the menu and number of sittings;
- the equipment used, for example, microwave ovens; and
- the amount of dishwashing. Disposable plates, etc. may be used.

THE DESIGN AND CONSTRUCTION OF EQUIPMENT

The hygienic design of equipment is necessary to comply with legislative requirements, avoid product contamination and to facilitate cost-effective cleaning and, if necessary, disinfection.

Poorly designed equipment, which cannot be dismantled, may be uncleanable, incapable of being chemically disinfected and may result in product contamination by pathogenic bacteria. Even if equipment can be dismantled, unhygienic design may make cleaning and disinfection prohibitively expensive.

The legal requirements

Food safety legislation requires all articles, fittings and equipment with which food comes into contact to:
- be kept clean;
- be so constructed, of such materials and maintained in such condition and repair as to minimize risk of contamination; and
- enable thorough cleaning and, where necessary, disinfection.

SUPERVISING FOOD SAFETY (LEVEL 3) **The design and construction of food premises and equipment**

Plan of a well-designed kitchen incorporating principles of continuous workflow and segregation of clean and dirty processes (not to scale).*

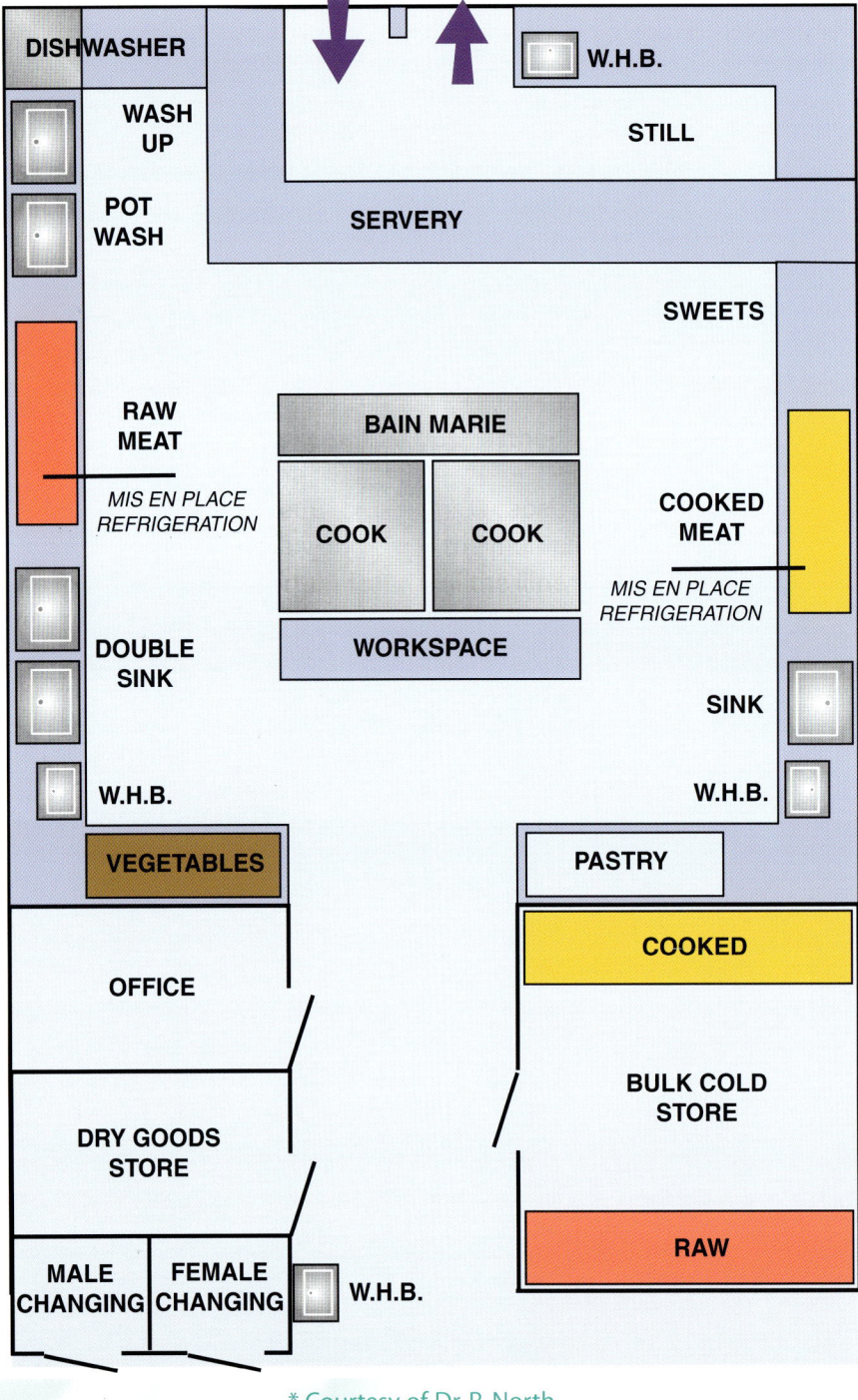

DISHWASHER		W.H.B.
WASH UP		STILL
POT WASH	SERVERY	
		SWEETS
RAW MEAT	BAIN MARIE	COOKED MEAT
MIS EN PLACE REFRIGERATION	COOK COOK	MIS EN PLACE REFRIGERATION
DOUBLE SINK	WORKSPACE	SINK
W.H.B.		W.H.B.
VEGETABLES		PASTRY
		COOKED
OFFICE		BULK COLD STORE
DRY GOODS STORE		
MALE CHANGING	FEMALE CHANGING W.H.B.	RAW

* Courtesy of Dr. R. North

Furthermore, equipment must be installed in a way which allows the surrounding area to be cleaned.

The Supply of Machinery (Safety) Regulations, 1992 (as amended in 1994)

The regulations require that new machinery used for preparing and processing foodstuffs carries a CE marking and must be designed and constructed to avoid health risks and in particular:

- contact materials of foodstuffs must satisfy the conditions set down in the relevant directives. Machinery must be designed and constructed to facilitate cleaning;
- all surfaces and joints must be smooth, without ridges or crevices which could harbour organic materials;
- projections, edges and recesses should be minimal. Continuous welding is preferable. Screws and rivets should not be used unless technically unavoidable;
- contact surfaces must be easily cleaned and disinfected. The design of internal surfaces, angles, etc. must allow thorough cleaning;
- cleaning residues must drain from equipment surfaces, pipework, etc., there must be no retention in voids;
- the design should prevent organic accumulations or insect infestation in uncleanable areas, e.g. by the use of castors or sealed bases; and
- lubricants must not come into contact with any product.

In addition, equipment manufacturers must provide accurate information on recommended products and methods of cleaning, disinfecting and rinsing. Equipment should be regularly maintained. Food must be removed prior to maintenance and the area cleaned after maintenance.

Construction materials

Materials in contact with food must be non-toxic, non-tainting and constituents from their surfaces must not migrate into the food or be absorbed by the food in quantities which could endanger health. Materials must have adequate strength over a wide temperature range, a reasonable life, be corrosion and abrasion resistant and be easily cleaned and disinfected. In most meat plants, the use of wood is forbidden except in rooms used for the storage of hygienically packed fresh meat.

The most widely used material is food-grade stainless steel. Some plastics may be suitable, but must be approved for food use. Aluminium should be avoided, as should copper and zinc. Handles of knives, brushes and other equipment should all be made from cleansable materials such as polypropylene or high-density stainless steel.

Surfaces should be smooth, non-porous, continuous, non-flaking and free from cracks, crevices and pits. Surfaces will need to retain a satisfactory finish throughout their life including anticipated abuse and normal wear and tear. Poor surfaces harbour grease, dirt and bacteria and are difficult to clean and disinfect. They may also result in physical contamination. Equipment that is damaged, chipped, cracked and pitted may need to be replaced. Temporary repairs with string or tape are unacceptable. Joints should be made by welding or continuous bonding to reduce projections, edges and recesses to a minimum. Soft wood is unsuitable as it is porous, cracks and splinters and is difficult to clean.

Equipment exterior

The external surfaces of equipment must avoid ledges and dust traps; for example, round legs are preferred to rectangular. It is important to avoid recessed corners, sharp edges, unfilled seams, uneven surfaces and hollows and projecting bolt heads, threads, screws or rivets that cannot be cleaned. Inaccessible spaces, pockets and crevices where product may accumulate must be absent.

Fixing and siting of equipment

Equipment must be sited so that there is sufficient space to facilitate access to all external and internal surfaces and, where required, to allow for rapid dismantling and reassembly. Machinery may be mounted on coved, raised platforms of concrete to facilitate cleaning. Where necessary, additional space may need to be provided. The bases and lower parts of machines, including motors and gears, may be difficult to clean and consequently collect dust and spillages which make ideal breeding sites for insects. Skirting or cover plates tend to trap dust.

Where practicable, and with due regard for safety, equipment can be mobile to facilitate its removal for cleaning. Gas and electricity supply pipes should be flexible and capable of being disconnected to facilitate cleaning. This will also enable adjacent wall surfaces and the floor to be effectively cleaned.

Mobile equipment

Drainage

All pipelines, vessels and equipment should be self-draining, not only to enable liquid deriving from foodstuffs to be discharged but also for cleaning and rinsing fluids. U-bends are fitted to sinks, toilets, etc. to stop odours and pests from the drains getting into food rooms.

Preparation surfaces

Preparation surfaces should be jointless, durable, impervious, the correct height and provide a firm base on which to work. If materials other than stainless steel are used, for example, food-grade plastic, care should be taken to seal the edges and gaps which may harbour food scraps. They must be able to withstand frequent and

SUPERVISING FOOD SAFETY (LEVEL 3) The design and construction of food premises and equipment

repeated cleaning and disinfection without any premature deterioration, pitting or corrosion.

Chopping boards

A variety of non-absorbent materials for chopping boards is now available, including good quality polypropylene. However, some are unsatisfactory. A good board should be durable and not split or warp and it is advantageous if it can be passed through a dishwasher. Boards should be non-toxic, difficult to score and resist stains, chemicals and heat.

Dishwashers should be used for cleaning and disinfecting chopping boards

As yet no ideal replacement has been found for hardwood chopping blocks. However, these should be maintained in good condition and used solely for chopping or sawing raw meat. A common colour-coding system for chopping boards involves using:

- **RED:** for raw meat
- **GREEN:** for salad
- **BLUE:** for fish
- **YELLOW:** for high-risk food
- **WHITE:** for dairy produce
- **BROWN:** for raw vegetables

Contamination

To avoid cross-contamination, it is important that the same equipment is not used for handling raw and high-risk products without being disinfected. To prevent the inadvertent use of equipment for high-risk and raw food the use of different colours and/or shapes is advantageous. Colour coding may be extended from knives and chopping boards to include washing facilities, trolleys, protective clothing, cloths and packaging material.

The cleaning of equipment

All operating instructions and procedures must be clearly communicated to the equipment users and cleaners. The equipment should be capable of being cleaned and, if necessary, disinfected safely, thoroughly and rapidly without the need for skilled fitters and specialized tools. If dismantling is necessary this must be achieved relatively easily, as should reassembly.

Sharp edges are a serious hazard for cleaners. A reluctance to clean equipment because of poor design will result in a lowering of hygienic standards. Hinges should be capable of being taken apart for cleaning. Angle iron is difficult to clean and tubular construction is preferred. Open ends to tubular legs must be sealed.

Key points

- Good design and the use of satisfactory building materials are essential to achieve high standards of hygiene.
- Clean and dirty (raw and high-risk) processes must be separated to minimize risk of contamination.
- Workflow must be continuous in a uniform direction from raw material to finished product.
- Surfaces and finishes must be non-toxic, non-flaking, durable and easy to maintain and clean.
- All food premises must have potable cold water supplies.
- Premises must be well lit and ventilated with satisfactory provision for drainage and waste management.
- Adequate facilities for handwashing, cleaning and disinfection must be provided.
- Equipment must be kept clean and in good condition to minimize risk of contamination.
- Colour coding of equipment assists in minimizing the risk of contamination.

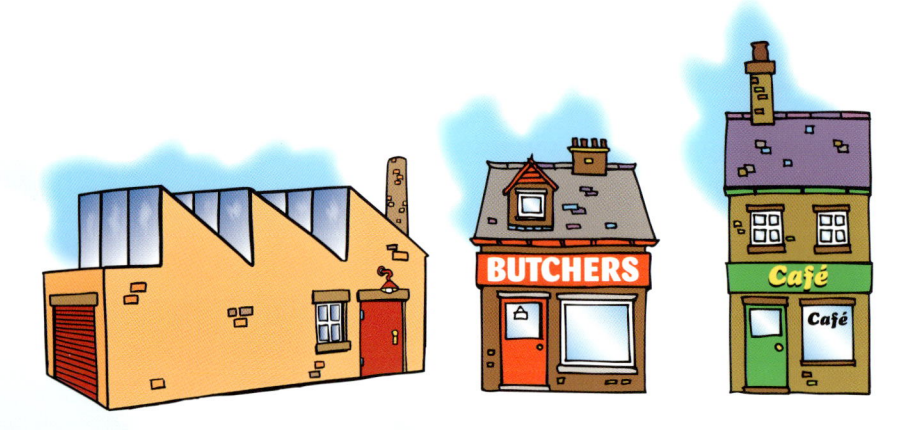

Food premises

9 Cleaning and disinfection

In any food business, soiling of both surfaces and equipment is unavoidable. The type and extent of soiling will vary considerably but, whatever the operation, it is essential that residues are not allowed to accumulate to levels which expose food to the risk of contamination.

The benefits of cleaning

Cleaning is an essential and integral part of a profitable food business. In addition to satisfying legal requirements, cleanliness will:
- disrupt routes of contamination, e.g. cleaning and disinfecting of tables used for raw and high-risk food;
- ensure a pleasant, safe and attractive working environment which will encourage effective working and reduce the risk of accidents to both staff and customers;
- promote a favourable image to the customer and assist in marketing the business;
- remove matter conducive to the growth of micro-organisms so facilitating effective disinfection and reducing the risk of food poisoning and spoilage;
- remove materials that would provide food or harbourage for pests and prevent early discovery of infestations;
- reduce the risk of foreign matter contamination and thereby obviate customer complaints;
- prevent damage to, or a reduction in, the efficiency of equipment and services, and reduce maintenance costs.

Problems caused by ineffective or negligent cleaning

Negligent cleaning may achieve a satisfactory physical appearance but can also result in hazardous bacterial contamination, for example, cleaning from raw to high-risk areas. Selection of the appropriate cleaning chemicals often requires expert technical advice as the use of the wrong chemicals, or the right chemicals at the incorrect strength, temperature or contact time, may have serious financial consequences. This not only applies to direct costs relating to product, equipment and premises but also, the cost of effluent treatment. It is also important that all cleaning chemicals are stored separate from food in a locked chemical store. Chemicals should never be stored in food containers and food should never be stored in used chemical containers. Ineffective or negligent cleaning may result in:
- microbiological hazards, contamination and a poor quality product which may lead to a reduction in shelf life, customer complaints, loss of reputation, court proceedings, food poisoning, redress from suppliers and loss of sales;
- wastage of food and production re-runs;

- chemical hazards, including taint and other forms of food contamination;
- corrosion and premature replacement of equipment;
- production breakdowns, for example, following the incorrect use of caustic soda which has removed grease from bearings;
- unacceptable deterioration of floor surfaces and drainage systems; and
- physical contamination hazards from worn and defective cleaning equipment.

Energy in cleaning

Cleaning is defined as 'the systematic application of energy to a surface or substance, with the intention of removing dirt'. Energy is available for cleaning in three distinct forms:

kinetic energy: physical – manual labour;
mechanical – machines;
turbulence – liquids
(cleaning in place);
thermal energy: hot water; and
chemical energy: detergents.

Normally, a combination of two or more energy forms is used. Manual labour is the most expensive and chemical energy the most economic, although adequate contact time is also important. The correct energy balance is essential for cost-effective cleaning.

Detergents

Detergents are chemicals, or mixtures of chemicals, made of soap or synthetic substitutes, which are used to remove grease or other soiling and promote cleanliness. They are available as powders, liquids, foams or gels. Detergents should be harmless to operatives and equipment, easy to rinse, have good wetting qualities, not form a scum, non-toxic, odourless and tasteless, i.e. non-tainting. If the temperature of water is too hot or there is insufficient detergent, food particles, especially protein, may be left on the plates after washing. The same may happen if plates are not pre-rinsed before loading them into a dishwasher.

Detergents have three important characteristics:
- **SURFACTANCY**, which reduces the surface tension of water and enables the detergent solution to penetrate dirt and grease;
- **DISPERSION**, which enables the detergent to lift the dirt from the surface; and
- **SUSPENSION**, which prevents the redeposition of the dirt so enabling it to be rinsed away.

Cost-effectiveness of the cleaning operation depends on the correct mix of the following:
- choosing the correct chemical;
- applying it at the optimum temperature and concentration;
- allowing it time to function; and
- using it with the correct equipment.

Washing soda is sometimes added to water to reduce surface tension.

Cleaning equipment

Consistent, high standards of cleanliness will only be achieved if the cleaning tools have been specifically manufactured for the stringent demands of the food industry. Correct choice is essential if operatives are to avoid recontamination of a cleaned surface with dirt or bacteria or, in the case of brushes, the contamination of product with bristles. The quality and cleanliness of tools which touch surfaces in direct contact with food is particularly important.

The use of colour coding for cleaning equipment, for example, handles of brushes, bristles and cloths used in high-risk situations, with different colours being used in raw and high-risk food areas, assists in reducing the risk of cross-contamination and reinforces hygiene training relating to the need to separate raw and high-risk food.

Abrasives, such as pumice, fine sand and chalk are occasionally used in cream cleansers to assist the removal of stubborn dirt.

Brushes

Brushes constructed from materials such as high-density polypropylene for stocks with bristles of polyester or rilsan give improved performance and resistance to wear. They are capable of withstanding boiling water and the normal cleaning chemicals used throughout the food industry. Wood and natural bristles must be avoided and worn-out brushes must be replaced. As brushes become worn they become less effective, they discolour and bristles are more likely to drop out. Blue coloured bristles are often preferred as they are more easily detected if they become loose. Nylon filaments are porous and quickly lose their stiffness in wet conditions, and inferior materials may even distort in hot water.

Mechanical equipment

These include floor scrubbers, rotating washers, power washers, air lines, steam cleaners, vacuum pick-ups and dishwashing and tray-cleaning machinery. Judicious use of mechanical equipment can significantly reduce labour requirements, but considerable care should be taken in selection to ensure that it is suitable for the use intended.

DISINFECTION

Although cleaning may remove large numbers of micro-organisms, it does not kill them. The

Gel or foam cleaning can improve performance

process which is used to destroy micro-organisms is known as disinfection. Normally, disinfection is carried out after cleaning, although sometimes the two processes are combined, when a sanitizer is used. A sanitizer is a detergent and disinfectant combined. It removes dirt and grease and reduces bacteria to a safe level. Sanitizers should only be used on physically clean or lightly soiled surfaces.

Disinfection is 'the destruction of micro-organisms, but not usually bacterial spores; it may not kill all micro-organisms but reduces them to a safe level. Sterilization is the process of destroying all micro-organisms, toxins and spores. Disinfection may be achieved by using heat, chemicals, irradiation or u/v radiation. The term sterilization relates to the destruction of all micro-organisms and spores and is normally unnecessary and impracticable to achieve within the food industry.

Heat disinfection

The application of heat is the most reliable and effective means of destroying micro-organisms, although it may not be the most practical, especially for surfaces. It is used in machines, such as dishwashing machines, with a water temperature of 88°C and a contact time varying from 15 to 90 seconds. It is also used in sterilizing units where articles may be fully immersed for a period of 30 seconds at 82°C.

Steam disinfection

Lances producing steam jets may be used to disinfect machinery or surfaces which are difficult to reach. Steam-cleaned equipment is self-drying.

Steam disinfection of a can opener

Choosing a chemical disinfectant

Disinfectants should not taint food and provided they are used in accordance with the manufacturers' instructions they should not have an adverse effect on surfaces or equipment or be toxic to staff or customers at the dilution level used. The amount and type of soiling, the type of detergent, the type of pathogen to be destroyed and the contact time available must all be considered.

Types of chemical disinfectants available include:
- chlorine release agents such as bleach; and
- quaternary ammonium compounds and alcohols.

Where to disinfect

Disinfection is usually only necessary for those surfaces where the presence of micro-organisms, at the levels found, will have an adverse effect on the safety or quality of the food handled. Disinfection or sanitizing should normally be restricted to:
- food-contact surfaces;
- hand-contact surfaces;
- cleaning materials and equipment;
- the surface of fruit and vegetables to be consumed raw; and
- the hands (only when essential).

As micro-organisms are rarely mobile and need to be physically carried onto food, the disinfection of non-food contact surfaces, such as floors and walls, is rarely necessary. Surfaces not directly coming into contact with food, but which are frequently touched by food handlers, need disinfecting to avoid the build-up of micro-organisms on hands.

SUPERVISING FOOD SAFETY (LEVEL 3) Cleaning and disinfection

Hand disinfection

Hand disinfection increases the risk of dermatitis and is only necessary in aseptic conditions or to protect food handlers such as fish filleters from developing septic cuts. In the majority of food handling situations frequently washing the hands properly in warm water, using a liquid soap will suffice. If hand disinfection is considered necessary it should be carried out after normal handwashing. Hand disinfectants should be fast-acting, dry rapidly and contain ingredients to protect the skin.

Disinfection of cleaning equipment and materials

Cleaning equipment is often an important vehicle of contamination and equipment used for hand or food contact surfaces should be disinfected frequently. Normal machine laundering at 65°C or above, in the case of cloths and towels, will achieve this. Floor mops should be thoroughly washed in hot water and detergent, squeezed to remove excess water and left to air dry. Wet mops should never be left in buckets or soaking in liquid overnight.

Disinfection frequency and effectiveness

As a general rule surfaces and equipment should be cleaned and disinfected immediately after use. Cleaning is easier when dirt and grease are fresh and this will avoid the build-up of bacteria and reduce the risk of cross-contamination. Furthermore it is part of 'clean as you go' which releases work areas and equipment for use. Disinfectants must be used at the correct dilution and temperature, as recommended by the manufacturer, and allowed sufficient contact time to destroy pathogens and spoilage organisms. Disinfectants are inactivated by food debris, dirt and detergent so it is essential that surfaces are cleaned and rinsed before using the disinfectant. Disinfectants must never be mixed with other chemicals. Effective of disinfecting is determined by bacteriological monitoring (swabbing), the use of ATP (adenosine triphosphate) or Vericleen, not visual inspection. Staff must use the appropriate protective clothing and equipment when handling chemicals.

PROCEDURES AND METHODS OF CLEANING

Whatever the location, industry, soiling type or circumstances, cleaning and disinfection comprises six basic stages:

- pre-clean: sweeping, wiping or scraping off loose debris, pre-rinsing and/or pre-soaking;
- main clean: applying detergent and loosening of the main body of dirt;
- intermediate rinse: removal of loosened dirt, chemical neutralization of cleaning agent residues;
- disinfection: destruction of residual micro-organisms;
- final rinse: removal of disinfectant residues; and
- drying: removal of final rinse water.

In the absence of visible soiling, the pre-clean may be omitted. The main clean and disinfection can take place in combination using specific chemicals known as sanitizers.

SUPERVISING FOOD SAFETY (LEVEL 3) Cleaning and disinfection

(This becomes a three-stage process, i.e. main clean/sanitize, rinse and dry. Where there is no risk of taint the rinse may be unnecessary.) Drying can either be natural, as in air drying, or physical, using disposable paper towels, hot air or a clean dry cloth.

Manual dishwashing

Manual dishwashing is only recommended for washing-up in catering premises, public houses and retail outlets selling high-risk foods, when suitable dishwashing machines are not available. It also applies to food-processing, packing and distribution plants where small items are handwashed. Thermal disinfection is most effective if double sinks are used but a suitable chemical disinfectant, such as hypochlorite in a tablet form may be used, to minimize condensation problems and health and safety risks. However, the rinse water should still be hot enough to allow air drying. The full, six-stage procedure should always be followed:

- remove any heavy or loose soil by scraping and rinsing in cold water;
- place articles in the first sink in detergent solution at 53°C to 55°C, scrub with a nylon brush and/or wipe with a clean cloth to loosen dirt residues, if temperatures are too high, e.g. 60°C+, proteins may be baked on and it will be too hot for hands;
- re-immerse in the first sink to wash off loosened dirt;
- place articles in the second sink to rinse off detergent;
- leave for sufficient time at a high enough temperature to ensure disinfection and rapid air drying, for example, 82°C for 30 seconds. Dilution (large volumes of water in sinks) will also aid disinfection. Baskets for disinfecting purposes should be maintained in good condition and inspected regularly. They should be loaded so that all surfaces of crockery and equipment are fully exposed to the rinse water. Hollow items such as cups should be placed on their side; and
- remove articles, allow to drain and evaporate dry on a clean, disinfected surface.

A rinse aid may be added to the rinse water to promote smear-free drying. Items should then be removed and stacked in a clean, protected area ready for re-use. Containers and pans should be stored inverted to minimize the risk of contamination.

Mechanical dishwashing

Mechanical dishwashing is preferable to, and often more economic than, manual washing, provided the machine is used according to the manufacturer's instructions. Machines, in addition to cleaning, are also a highly efficient means of disinfecting small items of equipment and should be used for articles such as the removable parts of slicing machines, polypropylene chopping boards and other items which come into contact with high-risk foods, provided that no damage to the item will result. The sequence is as follows:

- remove excess food into suitable waste bins; if necessary pre-soak or spray, unless the machine is fitted with a pre-wash cycle;
- pack articles in a neat, orderly fashion so that items do not overlap, place in the

machine and operate the wash cycle of hot detergent solution (49°C to 60°C), unless automatic;
- operate the rinse cycle (82°C to 88°C), with injection of rinse aid; and
- remove racks, allow cleaned items to drain and evaporate dry.

As a rule-of-thumb guide to the efficiency of a machine, if items coming out are too hot to handle and dry rapidly to a clean, smear-free finish, then the machine is operating correctly.

Better hygiene results are usually obtained from dishwashers compared to manual dishwashers because:
- machines use higher temperatures for washing and rinsing;
- stronger detergents can be used;
- there is always a hot water disinfection stage, unlike single sinks;
- the water does not get cooler or dirtier with use; and
- air drying of crockery and utensils is more likely.

To get the best results dishwashers should be well maintained and cleaned regularly. Food debris should be rinsed off before loading and dishwashers must be packed correctly and not overloaded.

Cleaning a cooked meat slicing machine

Pre-clean:
- switch off power socket and remove the plug;
- set the slice thickness control to zero;
- dismantle the machine, pre-clean and pass removed parts through the dish-washing machine. Alternatively, thoroughly clean removed parts in a sink using detergent and hot water at 55°C and then disinfect in second sink or using a chemical disinfectant. Where the machine is of a type that has a removable blade, a blade guard must be fitted before the blade is removed. Cleaning may then commence, with the proviso that no person may clean a slicer or other dangerous machine unless they have reached their eighteenth birthday and have been properly trained; and
- clean and disinfect the machine carriage using clean cloths, taking particular care with the electrical parts.

Post-clean:
- reassemble the machine very carefully to avoid possible accidents;
- disinfect parts handled or otherwise contaminated;
- check the guards are properly fitted, reconnect the power and switch on the machine. Test run to check safe working. This procedure is vital because accidents have been caused by guards having been improperly fitted after cleaning. If any adjustments have to be made, the machine should be switched off and disconnected and the test run repeated;

SUPERVISING FOOD SAFETY (LEVEL 3) Cleaning and disinfection

- switch off the machine, disconnect the plug and cover with a freshly laundered tea towel or other suitable covering; and
- supervisor to check.

Cleaning schedules

Cleaning schedules are essential to ensure effective cleaning and will assist a due-diligence defence. They must be clearly and concisely written, without ambiguity, to ensure that instructions to staff are easy to follow and result in the objective of the schedule being achieved.

Written schedules should specify:
- what is to be cleaned, e.g. ceilings, walls, floors, working surface, equipment, chopping boards, etc.;
- who is to clean it;
- when it is to be cleaned (frequency);
- how it is to be cleaned;
- the time necessary to clean it;
- the chemicals (and dilution), materials and equipment to be used, and the contact time necessary;
- the safety precautions to be taken;
- the protective clothing to be worn; and
- who is responsible for monitoring and recording that it has been cleaned.

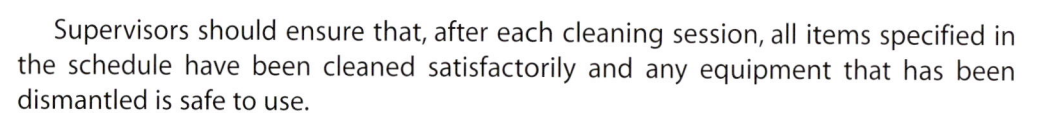

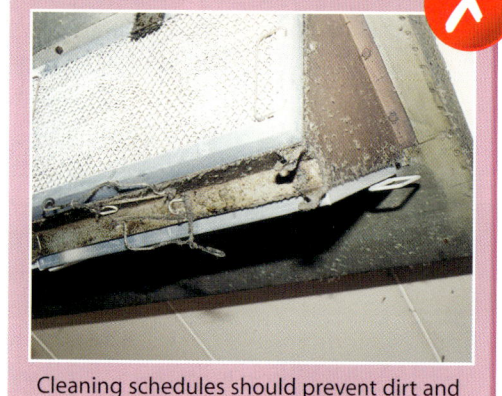

Cleaning schedules should prevent dirt and dust build-up and other cleaning problems

Supervisors should ensure that, after each cleaning session, all items specified in the schedule have been cleaned satisfactorily and any equipment that has been dismantled is safe to use.

The role of the supervisor in cleaning

Effective planning, supervision and organization is required to ensure coordinated and satisfactory cleaning. Supervisors must ensure that there are always sufficient cleaning materials and suitable facilities available and staff are given clear instructions and/or training on cleaning and using cleaning equipment. Staff can be motivated to clean if supervisors lead by example, demonstrate the correct way to clean and disinfect and monitor cleaning activities. Praise should be given for high standards and disciplinary action may be appropriate for unsatisfactory cleaning. Competency testing may be used to test knowledge and satisfactory implementation. Posters and notices may also be useful to encourage cleaning.

Supervisors will need to monitor the standard of cleaning by careful observation/inspection and occasionally using swabbing techniques such as ATP (adenosine triphosphate) or Vericleen which indicate the presence of food, dirt or bacteria in a few minutes and microbiological swabbing which provides results in several days. Cleaning schedules should also be checked to ensure they are being signed by the cleaner as they may be required for a due-diligence defence.

Regular auditing of the cleanliness of premises and equipment, including checking that cleaning schedules have been signed off by the supervisor will be necessary to verify that cleaning is effective. Monitoring the amount of cleaning chemicals used each week may also indicate the effectiveness of cleaning. Too little spent on chemicals indicates ineffective cleaning and too much may indicate wastage.

If the standards of cleaning are unsatisfactory the supervisor may need to:
- provide better training/instruction;
- provide more resources (time and/or materials/chemicals/equipment);
- provide closer supervision and increase frequency of monitoring;
- motivate staff to improve standards; and
- discipline staff for poor performance.

Key points
- Effective cleaning and disinfection of food premises and equipment is essential to secure food safety.
- Negligent cleaning results in cross-contamination and may be a contributory factor in food poisoning outbreaks.
- Detergents are used to remove dirt and grease.
- Disinfectants are used to reduce micro-organisms to a safe level.
- Staff involved in cleaning must be trained.
- Disinfection of food and hand-contact surfaces is essential.
- Cleaning equipment must be cleaned and disinfected after use.
- Cleaning schedules are essential to ensure effective cleaning and will assist a due-diligence defence.

10 Pest control

A food pest is a creature living on or in our food, which is capable of directly or indirectly contaminating food. They are destructive, noxious or troublesome.

Pest control is essential to prevent the spread of disease, although there are many other reasons for controlling pest infestations of food premises, including:
- to prevent the contamination of food by rodents or birds which may result in food poisoning. Rodents are scavengers and will feed on refuse, waste and unfit food. Rats often live in sewers and in close association with other animals. They often carry food poisoning bacteria, such as salmonellae, both inside and outside their bodies and on their feet and in their mouths. When entering food premises, they can easily transfer food poisoning bacteria to food and food-contact surfaces from their fur, feet, mouths, urine and droppings;
- to prevent contact with rat urine which may result in Weil's disease;
- to prevent the wastage of food by contamination, and losses due to pest damage of packaging;
- to avoid the costs associated with loss of production, recall of contaminated food or defending criminal or civil action as a result of selling contaminated products;
- to prevent damage caused by gnawing. Electrical fires, burst pipes and subsidence, caused by burrowing, may all result from rodent infestation;
- to comply with the law and avoid possible closure of the food business;
- to avoid losing customers who object to pest infested premises or the sale of contaminated food; and
- to avoid losing staff who will not want to work in infested premises.

The common pests found in the food industry include:
- rodents: rats and mice;
- insects: flies, wasps, cockroaches, psocids, silverfish, ants and stored product insects (moths, weevils and beetles) which infest dry products such as biscuits, cereals and flour;
- birds: mainly feral pigeons and sparrows and occasionally seagulls; and
- mites.

Cats and dogs may also be considered as pests and should not be allowed into food premises. They carry pathogens, including salmonella and campylobacter in their intestine and mouths and on their coats and paws. Contamination may also occur from droppings and urine.

Rodents

The two most common rodents encountered in food premises are the Brown Rat and the House Mouse. The Black Rat is rarely encountered.

The Norway Rat (Brown Rat)

This is the predominant rat in the United Kingdom. It usually lives in burrows in the soil, especially beneath buildings, but may also be found in sewers, food stores, on farms and rubbish dumps. The Norway Rat is omnivorous but prefers cereals. One pair of adult rats can produce hundreds of offspring within a year but fortunately many do not survive. It is essential to destroy lone invaders of food premises as a pair of established rats can soon become a major infestation.

The House Mouse

The House Mouse is normally found living in buildings which provide it with harbourage, warmth, food and nesting materials. The House Mouse is omnivorous and a pair of adult mice can produce 2,000 young within a year, with the help of their offspring.

Signs of rodent infestation

Certain members of staff should be specifically trained to identify evidence of pests. Cleaners are ideally suited for this purpose and should look for signs both inside and externally. Signs of infestation include:

- droppings: if very recent they are shiny and soft;
- the animals themselves, either dead or alive;
- gnawing marks and damage, for example, holes in sacks, teethmarks in food, nibbled packets;
- holes and nesting sites;
- rat runs in undergrowth or smears around pipes;
- smear marks from the animal's coat;
- the loss of small amounts of food;
- bait takes;
- smell; and
- footprints in dust.

Signs of infestation must be reported to the manager/supervisor immediately and any contaminated food must be discarded.

Insects

Insect pests can attack and destroy large amounts of food which becomes contaminated with bodies, webbing and excreta. Furthermore, cockroaches and flies may transmit food poisoning organisms to high-risk food. No food is completely safe from insect attack, but beans, cereals, flour and dried fruits are among the most susceptible to infestation.

Flies

Many types of fly can cause problems in the food industry including the Housefly, the Bluebottle and the Fruit Fly. Many pathogens have been isolated from flies, including salmonella, *E. coli* O157, campylobacter, listeria and rotavirus. Flies contaminate our food in four ways:

- to feed they vomit partly digested food from the previous meal;
- they continually defecate;
- they carry bacteria on the hairs on their body and legs; and
- pupal cases, eggs, maggots and dead bodies end up in our food.

Typical breeding sites for Houseflies are refuse and decaying organic matter. The female Housefly lays around 600 eggs and it takes less than two weeks to go from egg to maggot to pupa to adult in warm weather.

Blowflies usually breed on decaying matter of animal origin, especially meat.

Fruit Flies generally occur in bakeries or fruit canning factories and beer cellars, and some lay their eggs in unwashed milk bottles. Control usually involves removal of the breeding material.

Wasps

Wasps may contaminate food by transferring bacteria from their legs or bodies. They are a major nuisance in premises such as bakeries during the late summer.

The Wasp

Cockroaches

The two species of cockroach widely distributed in the United Kingdom are the Oriental Cockroach and the German Cockroach.

The Oriental Cockroach

The adults grow to about 24mm long and are shiny dark brown to black. They can climb rough vertical surfaces, such as brickwork, and are frequently found in cellars, kitchens,

The Oriental Cockroach

bakeries, hotels and drains. External survival and breeding, for example, in gardens, is possible.

The eggs are laid inside a case and take about two months to hatch at 25°C but this period is extended in cooler conditions. The female can produce over 150 eggs in its lifetime and it takes between six and 12 months to reach the adult stage in heated buildings with good food supplies.

The German Cockroach (Steam Fly)

The adult grows to about 15mm long and is yellowish brown. It can climb smooth painted walls and prefers the warm moist conditions found in kitchens, bakeries and especially ships' galleys. The female can produce around 300 eggs in its life span of three to 12 months.

Cockroach habits

Cockroaches live in groups and are omnivorous, nocturnal (active at night) insects that give off an unpleasant characteristic odour. During the day they usually hide in cracks, crevices, ducting, false ceilings, behind hot water pipes, electrical motors and behind skirtings and broken tiles and their presence is usually detected by faecal pellets or their smell. Neither species fly. Over 40 pathogenic organisms have been isolated from the bodies or droppings of cockroaches including food poisoning organisms, such as salmonella and *Cl. perfringens*.

Signs of insect infestation include:
- live or dead bodies;
- nymphs/moults;
- eggs, larvae and pupae;
- droppings, egg cases and smell (cockroaches); and
- webbing (moths).

Sticky traps may be used to detect the presence of pests.

Psocids or Booklice

Psocids are small (1mm to 2mm) cream, light brown or dark brown insects which are omnivorous and commonly infest flour, grain, nuts, chocolate, fish and meat products. They also feed on moulds and yeasts and infestations may be associated with packaging materials and pallets. The presence of booklice usually indicates conditions of high humidity.

Stored product insects

This is a large group of insects which attack foodstuffs in storage, transport and manufacture. It includes beetles, weevils, moths and their larvae. Dried products, cereals, flour, beans and nuts may all be attacked.

Pharaoh's Ant

Pharaoh's Ants are yellow/pale brown and approximately 2mm in length. Infestations usually occur in permanently heated buildings, especially hospitals, bakeries, hotels and residential property where they are often found in seemingly impenetrable food containers. All kinds of food may be attacked, although there is a preference for sweet and high protein food. Nests are difficult to detect and destroy. Physical transmission of pathogens to food is possible as they may visit drains, excreta and soiled dressings. Food is contaminated from their legs and bodies as well as droppings.

Bird pests

Birds which commonly gain access to food premises are sparrows, feral pigeons and starlings. Gulls are becoming an increasing problem, though rarely enter buildings. Warehouses and large food factories are prime targets although bakeries and supermarkets may also be affected. Pathogens associated with birds include salmonella and campylobacter.

Reasons for control
- to prevent the contamination of food or equipment by droppings, bodies, feathers and nesting materials;
- to prevent the transmission of food poisoning organisms;
- to remove sources of insect and mite infestation provided by nests, excreta and the birds themselves;
- to prevent blockages of gutters which may result in flooding and expensive maintenance;
- to prevent defacement of buildings (bird droppings produce an acid which attacks stone);
- to prevent roosting on fire escapes and similar structures, which may result in a safety hazard for human occupants; and
- to prevent damage to food packaging.

Pest control

Every food business should carry out integrated pest management, i.e. a control programme involving a series of integrated measures to control pests. Pests require warmth, food, shelter, a nesting place and security. Food premises provide all of these. Denial of these factors is known as environmental control and is the first and most important control measure intended to prevent infestation.

Environmental (preventive) control
Environmental control may be considered as denial of:
- access – by design, maintenance and proofing of buildings; and
- food and harbourage – by good housekeeping.

Design, maintenance and proofing of buildings
Pests gain access to food premises in various ways. They may enter through open windows or doors, through gaps and cavities in the structure of the building or they may be brought in with food, packaging material or even laundry. Buildings must be designed and maintained to avoid undisturbed areas which can provide harbourage for pests. False ceilings, boxing, ducting, ovens and elevators must always be accessible

SUPERVISING FOOD SAFETY (LEVEL 3) **Pest control**

for inspection and treatment. Cavities in internal walls or between surface finishes and walls must be eliminated or effectively sealed. Service pipes or conduits passing through walls should be cemented in position.

All structural damage which provides access for pests must be repaired immediately and gaps around pipework must be sealed. Drains should be provided with suitable covers and defective drains should be made good.

Poor maintenance will allow pest entry

All buildings should be adequately proofed; doors should be self-closing and provided with metal kick plates, ventilation stacks should be provided with wire balloons and all ventilation openings, including opening windows (where there is a risk of infestation) must be adequately proofed to avoid pests gaining access. If a pencil can pass through a gap so can a young mouse. Air curtains are occasionally used to keep out flying insects.

All sources of water, such as dripping taps, defective gutters and leaks should be repaired and puddles removed.

Good housekeeping

If a pest breaches the first stage of the defences, i.e. proofing and maintenance, as well as inspection of raw materials, then good housekeeping will reduce the risk of the lone invader becoming a major infestation. In particular, it is important to ensure that:

- premises are kept in a clean and tidy condition to reduce sources of food, harbourage and nesting material;
- cleaners do not remove or reposition bait boxes;
- spillages are cleared away promptly and food is not left outside;
- food is kept in pest-proof containers and lids are always replaced;
- stock is stored and rotated correctly;
- undisturbed areas of unused equipment are checked frequently;
- adequate provision is made for the disposal of waste and areas are kept clean and tidy with tight-fitting lids being provided and used;
- as far as practicable, areas around the premises are kept free of harbourage and pests. Vegetation should be cut back;
- all raw materials, including food, packaging and equipment, are checked to ensure they are not bringing pests into the premises;
- storage areas are regularly inspected and cleaned. Goods should be stored off the floor in well-lighted and ventilated areas. Old stock and new stock should, as far as practicable, be segregated; and
- staff are alert and well trained. Regular audits are undertaken.

The regular inspection of the food premises by a pest control contractor to ensure satisfactory environmental control is important to minimize risk of infestation.

Physical and chemical control methods are necessary when environmental control has not succeeded. In order to control pests successfully you need to know the species involved, the size and location of the infestation and the source of the pests.

Physical control methods

Physical control methods are usually preferred as the pest is caught, either dead or alive, and consequently is not able to die in some inaccessible place and the dead body will not contaminate food. Furthermore, physical control methods can be used during food production. Examples of physical control include:

- rodent traps (baited or unbaited);
- electronic flying-insect killers (EFKs) which use ultra-violet (u/v) light to attract insects. Insects are caught on glue boards or electrocuted on charged grids. Catch trays for dead insects should be emptied frequently. EFKs should never be positioned above food or food equipment, next to a window (may attract insects if left open) or near fluorescent tubes, as they emit u/v light;
- sticky cockroach traps or pheromone traps for moths and wasps. These are useful for monitoring the extent of infestations and the success of chemical treatments;
- mist nets for birds; and bird scaring devices.

Catch trays must be emptied frequently

Deliveries should be checked to ensure they are pest free. Stock, especially in dry stores, should be examined regularly and any infested stock segregated and removed from the premises immediately.

Chemical control methods

Unfortunately, although physical control methods may catch the occasional invader, they are usually unsuitable for dealing with major pest infestations, which have to be destroyed as quickly as possible.

Rodenticides, chemicals for killing rodents, are used in bait boxes. Modern formulations can be provided in solid blocks or in a paste formulation to avoid problems from spillage and reduce the risk of food contamination.

The key to effective chemical control is to identify the insect and then determine which is the most vulnerable stage in its life cycle. Knock-down and residual insecticides of low toxicity can be used to control insects. Before use, all food and, where practicable, equipment, should be removed and after treatment, work surfaces must be thoroughly cleaned and pests removed before food production commences. Particular care is necessary to avoid food contamination by dead flies or insecticide if aerosol fly spray is used by food handlers. (Indiscriminate control by food handlers is not good practice.) Insecticide will not be broken down by cooking so even raw food contaminated by pesticide should be discarded.

A range of insecticidal dusts, baits, gels and sprays may be used to control most pests if care is taken to avoid contamination of food. Most treatments rely on the insects walking over the formulation and ingesting or absorbing a lethal dose. The continuous use of residual insecticides is not recommended in food rooms because of the risk of dead insects dropping into food. However, they may be useful in non-food rooms.

Ant and wasp nests should be located and destroyed by the pest control operator.

Fumigation of product is usually the only successful way to control infestations within commodities, although severe infestations may require the destruction of the product because of contamination with dead bodies.

Narcotizing of birds using alphachloralose, which is a stupefying substance, may be successful as any protected species can be released and the pest species collected and humanely destroyed.

It is essential that chemical control is undertaken by trained staff from either local authorities or specialist contractors. Safety precautions must be taken to comply with health and safety legislation. As soon as an infestation is discovered, immediate advice must be obtained and a pest control contractor will probably need to be contacted immediately.

The use of a pest control contractor

When selecting a pest control company, apart from the cost of the service, the following points should be taken into consideration:
- the type of pests you wish to control and the company's competency to deal with them;
- the ability to give 24-hour cover and provide an emergency call-out service;
- the use of suitably trained and discreet staff, with experience of the food industry;
- the frequency of the visits;
- the methods and materials to be used;
- if the company is a member of an appropriate professional association;
- the ability to provide a written report, including recommendations; and
- the adequacy of appropriate insurance cover regarding product, public and employees' liability.

The employment of a contractor does not absolve the company from overall responsibility for the conditions of the premises and food. However, it would most likely assist if a due-diligence defence was being relied upon.

SUPERVISING FOOD SAFETY (LEVEL 3) Pest control

BROWN RAT

BABY HOUSE MICE

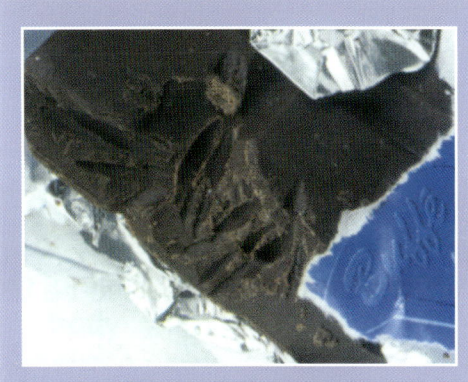

RODENT TEETH MARKS

RODENT DAMAGE

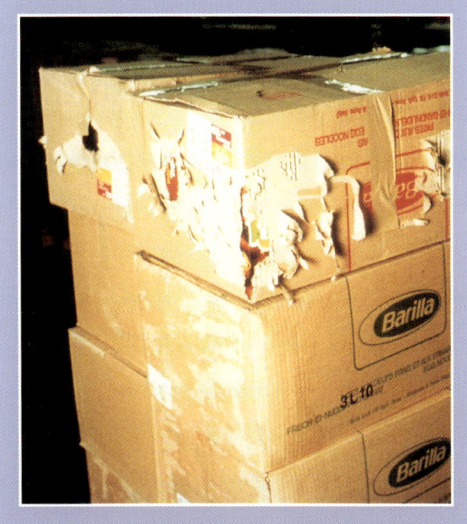

RODENT DAMAGE

SPILLAGE RESULTING FROM RODENT DAMAGE OF SACKS

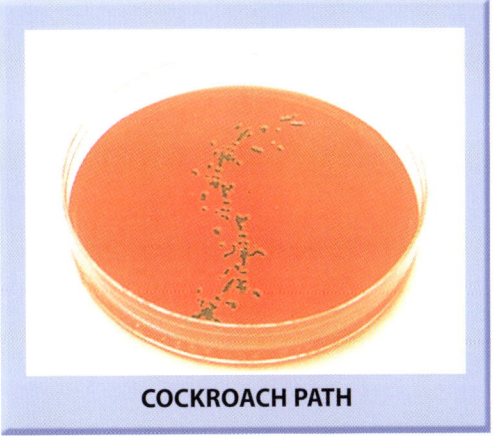

SUPERVISING FOOD SAFETY (LEVEL 3) Pest control

GERMAN COCKROACH

COCKROACH PATH

ORIENTAL COCKROACH

COCKROACH TRAP

(A) FERAL PIGEON

(B) SPARROW

LARDER BEETLES AND LARVAE

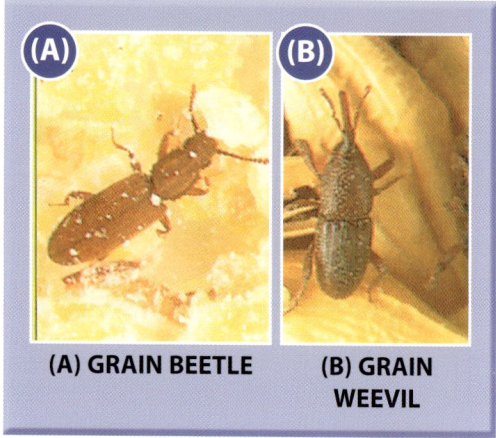

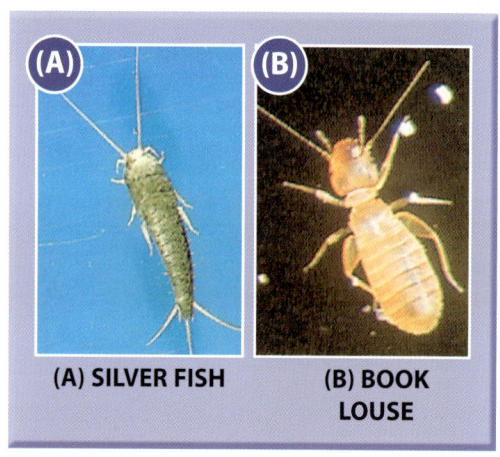

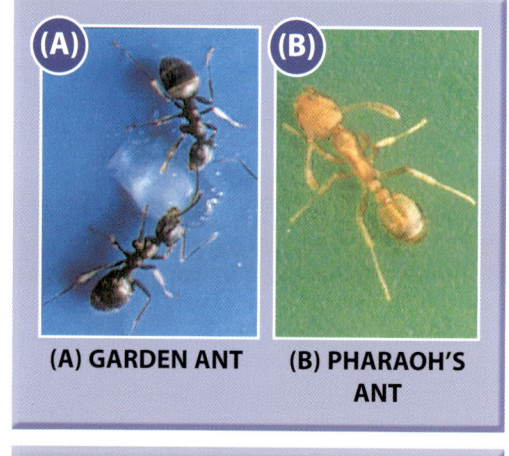

SUPERVISING FOOD SAFETY (LEVEL 3) Pest control

LARVA OF FLOUR BEETLE

(A) GRAIN BEETLE

(B) GRAIN WEEVIL

(A) SILVER FISH

(B) BOOK LOUSE

(A) GARDEN ANT

(B) PHARAOH'S ANT

MILL MOTH

MILL MOTH LARVA

A due-diligence defence

In order to demonstrate due diligence with regard to pest control it will be necessary to demonstrate:

- the presence of an effective pest control system;
- the absence of previous complaints;
- the pest control book is accurately completed and that all essential recommendations have been acted on;
- regular inspections by a reputable contractor have been carried out;
- staff are trained to recognize and report signs of pests;
- deliveries are checked for the presence of pests;
- effective proofing and control measures are in place, for example, electric fly killers; and
- good housekeeping and satisfactory maintenance.

The role of the supervisor in pest control

Supervisors and their staff should be able to recognize signs of pests and know the action required in the event of an infestation or a complaint regarding contamination of a food product by pests.

The supervisor should contact their pest control contractor as soon as they are aware of a problem. The contractor should be accompanied throughout the inspection. The supervisor should record the position of all bait boxes and any recommendations regarding proofing, good housekeeping or control should be carried out as quickly as possible.

Regular audits should be undertaken to verify that the integrated pest management system is effective. The audit should ensure that:

- deliveries are checked for signs of pests and contaminated deliveries are rejected;
- the premises are proofed against the entry of pests;
- the housekeeping is satisfactory;
- there are no signs of pests;
- the rodent control book is up to date and all recommendations acted on;
- bait boxes are in place and untouched; and
- physical control methods are operating effectively, especially, electric fly killers. These should be positioned correctly, u/v tubes replaced annually and catch trays emptied regularly.

Key points

- Rats, mice, flies and cockroaches are the most common pests of food premises.
- Pests can spread foodborne diseases.
- Infestations of pests may result in serious food complaints, prosecutions and the closure of the food business.
- Staff must be trained to identify evidence of pests which should be reported immediately.

SUPERVISING FOOD SAFETY (LEVEL 3) Pest control

- Environmental controls, i.e. preventing access and good housekeeping are the most cost-effective way of preventing infestations.
- Physical controls are preferred to avoid food contamination.
- Chemical controls should be applied by specialists.
- Integrated pest management is the key to successful control.

*All pest photographs used in this book were provided courtesy of Anticimex (Sweden) and Rentokil Initial plc.

Mouse baked in loaf

11 Supervisory management

Supervisors and middle managers are an essential link in maintaining high standards of hygiene and preventing food poisoning. Their most important role is to ensure that food safety policies are implemented and the company's aims and objectives are achieved. Supervisors must communicate standards and ensure that staff are aware of their responsibilities. They should provide effective supervision, including motivation, instruction and on-the-job training to develop competency and control. Supervisors have a key role in the successful implementation of HACCP, or other food safety management systems. They must ensure that hazards are controlled, monitoring is effective and corrective action is taken in the event of failures. Supervisors should advise management when standards are being formulated and, in particular, ensure management are aware of the resources necessary to achieve the required standards.

Supervisors must be knowledgeable about good hygiene practices, the food safety management (HACCP) system implemented by their business, and company policy and legal requirements.

They will need the skills to lead by example, select new staff, train effectively, be able to prepare and implement company hygiene policy and be able to control, monitor and correct staff and audit the business. Good communication and motivational skills are also essential. Staff should be encouraged to operate hygienically; good hygiene practice should be praised and bad hygiene may result in disciplinary action.

Standards

Standards are necessary to ensure consistency and to provide a reference point to determine when a target has been achieved or a task, such as cleaning, has been completed satisfactorily. The term 'standard' may be used in several different ways. Voluntary standards, for example, hygiene or cleanliness, may be arbitrary levels; legal standards, such as storage temperatures for food, and international standards such as HACCP and ISO 9000. Hygiene standards should be communicated to staff by supervisors.

Standards may be set by an individual, a company, customers, governments, trade associations and independent standards authorities. Premises with high standards develop a good reputation, which attracts new customers, with the minimum number of complaints. Food safety standards set above the minimum legal level will ensure compliance with the law, codes of practice and industry guides and the production of safe, wholesome food of acceptable quality and shelf life. Standards are also essential to facilitate control, monitoring and auditing to assess compliance. The best way to check standards is to implement a systematic monitoring programme.

Specifications are documented standards which describe the safety and quality characteristics of the raw materials and the products obtained from suppliers.

Specifications ensure uniformity and may include minimum standards for weight, size, colour, pH, a_w, absence or maximum numbers of micro-organisms, processing requirements, delivery details, including temperature, absence of physical and chemical contaminants, packaging and labelling. They may also detail the action that will be taken, usually rejection, if the specification is not adhered to.

Food safety policies

When a company has determined its aim and objectives, the standards can be determined and incorporated into a food safety policy. The food safety policy can be used to attain good hygiene practices or good manufacturing practices which are essential prerequisites to the effective implementation of HACCP based systems. This document is also very useful to support a due-diligence defence and legal compliance. It is an effective way of communicating the required standards to staff and identifying training needs. To remain effective, the document should be reviewed regularly. A responsibility flow chart showing management structure and individual responsibilities with regard to hygiene should be included, together with the following:

- a commitment to produce safe food;
- a commitment to observe all relevant legal requirements, industry guides to good hygiene practice and government codes of practice;
- a commitment to identify hazards and implement effective control and monitoring procedures, especially at points critical to food safety and to review the hazard analysis system periodically and whenever the operations of the food business change;
- staff training and the implementation of a planned food hygiene training programme (training records should be maintained);
- procedures to ensure that all food and water suppliers are satisfactory/approved (suppliers should provide a copy of their food safety policy and customer references);
- a commitment to provide the necessary premises, equipment, facilities and maintenance to achieve high standards of hygiene, including personal hygiene;
- satisfactory temperature control and monitoring systems for food ingredients and products during storage, preparation/processing, distribution and display. Procedures should be identified for safe alternatives if equipment is defective;
- systems to ensure satisfactory cleaning and, where necessary, disinfecting of the premises, equipment and facilities (cleaning schedules will be required);
- adequate pest control measures, including proofing, the use of specialist contractors and maintaining records;
- effective waste management, including the satisfactory internal and external storage of waste, the cleaning of receptacles, the frequency of emptying, and the provision and cleaning of impervious hard-standings;
- procedures and systems for health screening and the reporting of staff illness, dealing with visitors, contractors, enforcement officers, food poisoning

incidents, customer complaints, delivery of raw materials, traceability and product recall, hazard warnings and waste management;
- effective quality assurance/control systems, including stock rotation, foreign-body control, organoleptic assessment, sampling, food labelling and in-house audits. Procedures for removing unacceptable suppliers from the approved list; and
- a commitment to provide the resources for, and training of managers to ensure, the implementation, updating and enforcement of the policy throughout the business.

Communication and motivation

An essential role of supervisors is to communicate standards, company hygiene rules and legal responsibilities to staff. This starts with induction training but is a continuous process to keep staff up to date and reinforce good hygiene practice. There are several techniques that can be used to make staff aware of the requisite standards, including:

- effective verbal or written instruction, demonstrating good practice and testing;
- placing new employees with an experienced 'buddy';
- the use of training courses, DVDs, videos, e-learning, coaching cards or distance learning;
- using an external consultant or environmental health practitioner/officer;
- using team briefings or memoranda, either individually or on notice boards;
- issuing a booklet of hygiene rules to all new staff;
- using posters and notices; and
- leading by example.

Once staff are aware of the required standards they must be motivated to implement them continuously. Motivation starts by explaining the importance of hygiene standards, not only for the business but for the individual. Nobody wants to be responsible for causing a food poisoning outbreak, especially if this results in them losing their job.

The importance of good hygiene practice can be demonstrated by supervisors and managers leading by example, by correcting staff who do things wrong and by rewarding staff who do things right. This can be in the form of praise or even 'hygiene employee of the month'. Staff who continuously demonstrate bad hygiene practices should never be promoted and may be disciplined or even dismissed.

Observation and monitoring of good hygiene practices reinforces their importance as does routine questioning and competency testing.

Quality assurance

Quality assurance may be considered as all the planned and systematic actions necessary to provide confidence that a product or service will satisfy the customer's requirements for quality over time. Many organizations have developed their own quality assurance systems and some of these may comply with the International Standards Organisation ISO 9000 series. Recognition for achieving the standard is through accredited certification bodies.

Quality assurance is proactive and attempts to stop things going wrong in the first place. It is a continuous process of product assessment and fault correction throughout production and should be the responsibility of all staff. The effective implementation of quality assurance requires:
- the specification (what is to be done);
- documented instruction (how it is to be done);
- the recording system (to confirm it has been done); and
- a monitoring system (to confirm recording and corrective actions are satisfactory).

Quality control

Quality control is differentiated from quality assurance in that it is a series of techniques used to assess compliance with a standard specification by testing and product sampling. It is usually based on statistical criteria and often occurs on completion of production. In essence, it is a reactive process which identifies things that are wrong after the event and does not necessarily determine the cause of the problem.

Quality must be built into a food product - it cannot be inspected into it.

The inspection/audit of food premises

An inspection of a food premises or operation will only be effective if the person undertaking the inspection has a clear understanding of the reason for inspection and also has the relevant technical knowledge, skills and experience. The inspection must be planned and sufficient time must be allowed to achieve the objective. After the inspection, the data collected will need to be analyzed to determine the action to be taken to rectify any defects. A comprehensive report should be written and problems must be followed up to ensure compliance. An inspection involves careful observation and examination whereas an audit may be considered as comparing what you actually do with what you say you do. The two processes will usually overlap. Supervisors should prepare for audits by collecting all relevant records.

Knowledge required

The inspector must have a thorough understanding of:
- all technical aspects of the operation, for example, catering practice, cook-chill or canning;
- the legal requirements and relevant codes of practice or industry guides;
- the main causes of food poisoning and complaints associated with the type of operation;
- all relevant aspects of HACCP; and
- the industry norm, i.e. standards expected for similar premises.

Purpose of the inspection/audit
There are many different reasons for inspecting a premises, including:
- to ensure that the premises/operation is capable of producing safe food;
- to assess the effectiveness of HACCP, especially in relation to critical control points (verification);
- to ensure policies and procedures are being adhered to and standards are being achieved;
- to identify the training needs of staff;
- to provide advice;
- to demonstrate management commitment to food safety;
- to respond to a complaint; and
- to re-visit.

Stages in the inspection
(1) Planning and preparation
When the objectives of the inspection have been decided, the scope and depth can be determined. The inspection may consider microbiological, chemical and physical hazards and it may be a full or part inspection or very specific.

The equipment required will include a probe thermometer, torch, protective clothing, sample bags, a scraper and an A4 pad and clipboard. The inspector may need additional knowledge and training to develop inspection skills, including interviewing, simulation/reconstruction, measurement, analyzing and report writing.

Prior to undertaking the inspection, it is useful to have records of previous inspections, specifications, hazards, risks, relevant legislation, industry guides and codes of practice. Access to monitoring records relating to customer complaints, pests and cleaning, together with the HACCP plan and site layout, would also be beneficial. To be effective, checklists should be designed specifically for the premises being inspected, although *aides-memoires* may be even more useful.

(2) Conducting the inspection
The timing of the inspection will be dictated by the objective. If undertaking a comprehensive inspection, it is necessary to examine each step in the production of food from the receipt of deliveries to the serving of customers. The hazards (contamination, multiplication and survival) controls, monitoring and corrective action at each stage (critical control point) should be considered.

Observations should be carried out as inconspicuously as possible and the inspection should be methodical. A typical routine involves starting at a defined point, such as the wash-hand basin, within a room, the progressive examination of all relevant items around the perimeter and then the same ordered examination of central fittings, installation or equipment.

The inspection should be thorough. Every aspect of the subject under examination should be covered. It may not be enough to look at a piece of equipment; it may need to be dismantled and/or moved from its position. Cupboards and refrigerators may need to be wholly or partially emptied and surfaces may need to be scraped or tapped to assess soundness. In this respect, full use should be made of the senses: sight, smell, hearing and touch.

(3) Analysing the data

All of the raw data collected during the inspection will need careful analysis to provide meaningful information which can be presented in the report. For example: several cleaning defects in differing rooms may indicate inappropriate cleaning schedules; if staff are wearing dirty protective clothing this may result from poor communication and/or poor supervision or training; several empty paper towel or soap dispensers may demonstrate ineffective monitoring as well as poor management commitment to achieving high standards of personal hygiene; food hygiene certificates may be hung on the wall, but the staff may not be competent to undertake their activities and to produce safe food.

(4) Report

The report of the inspection should be more than just a list of faults. Good practice and achievements should be complimented. Faults should be grouped together, for example, personal hygiene or cleaning. The remedial work should be prioritized, for example, an unsafe process should be dealt with at the time of the inspection, some cleaning problems may need to be rectified within a day, whereas some decoration, structural items or replacement equipment may be dealt with in one to three months.

Recommendations and legal requirements should be clearly distinguished, and any solutions proposed should be cost-effective and practical.

Inspection by an authorized officer

In the event of an inspection by an authorized officer, the supervisor or manager should make the officer welcome and answer his/her questions accurately and honestly. A plan of the premises should be available, together with all relevant monitoring records. The officer will be interested in the food safety policy and HACCP documentation provided, including cleaning schedules, training records, temperature control, delivery details and pest control. The officer may wish to speak to particular members of staff, who should be made available.

It is usual for the officer to be accompanied throughout the inspection. If you do not understand the reason for a request or, for example, why a particular process is considered to be a risk, you should always ask for an explanation.

At the conclusion of the inspection, it is advisable to keep a record of any work that must be completed immediately and also the follow-up action, if any, the officer intends to take. Priorities and timescales for completing any remedial work should be noted.

The manager may wish to use inspections by the environmental health practitioner/officer to improve hygiene standards. Staff should be advised why the officer is inspecting the premises. He/she should reinforce the good hygiene practices required by staff, for example, wear clean protective clothing and wash his/her hands on entering the food room. The officer could be asked to speak to individual members of staff to emphasize the importance of hygiene, address all the staff or undertake a training session.

Staff training
The objectives of hygiene training
The main objective of hygiene training is to change the behaviour and attitude of food handlers at work and so minimize the risk of food poisoning and food complaints. To achieve this objective, staff will need to be provided with the knowledge and skills to operate hygienically and then motivated and supervised to ensure that they implement what they have learned. Training should not be undertaken haphazardly but must be carefully planned. The most effective way of undertaking hygiene training is to develop and implement a training programme, the principles of which are applicable to all businesses, although the programme will be less formal for smaller businesses.

The benefits of hygiene training
Training contributes significantly to the profitability of a food business by:
- assisting in the production of safe food and reducing the risk of food poisoning;
- safeguarding the quality of the product and reducing food wastage;
- reducing complaints;
- generating a pride in appearance and practices, increasing job satisfaction and probably reducing staff turnover;
- contributing to increased productivity;
- ensuring that all the correct procedures, including cleaning, are followed;
- complying with any legal provisions or the requirements of industry guides or codes of practice (providing a due-diligence defence);
- promoting a good company image which should result in increased business; and
- improving the supervisory skills of managers.

Induction training
Induction training of all food handlers is particularly important, in addition to some of the above general benefits it will:
- ensure new staff are aware of the company hygiene rules;
- comply with specific requirements of the industry guides/legislation;
- demonstrate the importance the business places on food hygiene, thereby contributing to the right culture;
- reduce the need for close supervision;
- reduce the amount of waste food;
- minimize the risk of bad hygiene practices developing; and
- ensure staff are aware of their legal obligations and reduce the risk of prosecution.

SUPERVISING FOOD SAFETY (LEVEL 3) Supervisory management

Refresher training

Refresher training should be continuous to ensure food handlers always implement the good hygiene practices they have been taught. It reinforces hygiene rules and demonstrates management commitment to food hygiene. The supervisor has a key role in refresher training and they should never let a member of staff break a hygiene rule without correcting it. Bad habits must not be allowed to develop.

Refresher training is also important to keep staff up to date with the latest food safety information as well as the operation of new equipment.

Training methods

There are many ways of ensuring that food handlers are effectively trained depending on the type of business, their level of hygiene knowledge and their literary skills. Continuous on-the-job instruction and control by a knowledgeable supervisor is essential. A large number of visual aids are available to enhance training sessions or reinforce important messages. Videos, overhead transparencies, books, leaflets, posters and computer-based training packages are all useful, especially if the audience finds them enjoyable. Humorous illustrations are more memorable than text. Interactive training packages and training sessions, for example, group exercises, quiz books, software, games and role playing, produce better results.

The legal requirement for training

Food business operators are to ensure that:
- food handlers are supervised and instructed and/or trained in food hygiene matters commensurate with their work activity, in other words, trained to carry out their specific job safely and ensure the production of safe food; and
- those responsible for the development and maintenance of the food safety management system based on the HACCP principles, or for the operation of the relevant guides have received adequate training in the application of the HACCP principles.

It is recommended that:
- all food handlers receive written or verbal instruction in the essentials of food hygiene before they start work and additional hygiene awareness instruction (introduction to food hygiene in Scotland) within four weeks of starting work;
- food handlers who prepare open high-risk foods or have a supervisory role receive Foundation/Elementary (Level 2) training within three months of starting work; and
- supervisors undertake Intermediate training (12 to 24 hours) or Advanced (Level 4) training (24 to 40 hours duration), depending on their actual duties. Supervisors and managers should also undertake relevant HACCP training.

Training programme and records

It is good practice for food businesses to have a training programme which identifies the training needs of each food handler. Records of training, to include induction (hygiene essentials), hygiene awareness, Foundation/Elementary (Level 2),

Intermediate (Level 3) or Advanced (Level 4), any specific courses attended, such as HACCP, and refresher training, should be completed for each food handler to assist compliance with the legal requirements and to assist in establishing a due-diligence defence. (It must always be remembered that the law requires competency for food handlers to produce safe food, not an ageing certificate on the wall). Records are also useful to provide evidence that staff have received appropriate training, to identify training needs and plan a training programme.

Verification of effective training

Training can be considered successful when food handlers implement the highest standards of food hygiene at all times, even when there is no supervisor present. Verification therefore involves ensuring staff have the knowledge and implement this knowledge. Verification also includes observing staff and auditing their activities, for example, that the refrigerator is correctly loaded and that all necessary records are satisfactorily completed. Staff could be asked to complete written or verbal tests but more importantly they should be given competency tests. Staff must, for example, be able to demonstrate how to wash their hands correctly or use a probe thermometer safely. Accurately completed training records should be available.

THE INVESTIGATION OF FOOD POISONING OUTBREAKS

The effective investigation of food poisoning outbreaks is essential to limit the spread of infection and to provide information:

- for the food industry on unsafe products and practices;
- to improve the effectiveness of inspections by enforcement officers; and
- to use when formulating new legislation.

A general outbreak involves two or more persons from different households. A household outbreak involves two or more persons in the same household but not connected to another case or outbreak.

In the event of a serious or large outbreak, an outbreak control team is usually established. A food poisoning outbreak control team consists of several experts, including a consultant in public health, medicine, a microbiologist and an environmental health practitioner/officer.

The objectives of an investigation are to:

- contain the spread of illness and prevent further outbreaks (main objectives);
- identify the outbreak location (place where food vehicle was prepared or served);
- identify the food vehicle (food eaten which gave rise to the illness) and prevent further sales;
- identify the causative agent involved, for example, *Salmonella* Enteritidis, Norovirus, a poisonous chemical or a toxic plant;
- trace cases/carriers, especially food handlers;
- trace the source of the causative agent;
- determine the main faults that contributed to the outbreak, for example, food

left at ambient temperatures for several hours;
- make recommendations to prevent recurrence; and
- provide data for use in surveillance.

The role of the environmental health practitioner/officer

In addition to his/her involvement with the outbreak control team, the environmental health practitioner/officer uses his/her skills in tracing cases and persons at risk, organizing the collection of specimens and interviewing people involved to obtain information to assist with achieving the above objectives.

When the outbreak location has been identified, the investigating officer will undertake a comprehensive investigation and inspection of the operation to ascertain the faults in the food preparation and the management failures that resulted in the faults. If the evidence suggests the sale of unfit food and the absence of a due-diligence defence, the officer may also collect evidence for use in legal proceedings.

The officer will need to secure the assistance of the manager and/or supervisor to assist in the investigation. In the event of a very recent outbreak, the officer will request the suspension of cleaning and disinfection and, perhaps, the termination of food production or even the closure of the food premises.

The officer will require details of:
- customers, especially other cases;
- all food production staff and their functions;
- records, especially staff sickness, including staff with septic cuts or boils; and
- all relevant food production details.

The officer may require samples of food and meal or packaging remains. Swabs of surfaces and equipment may be taken. Staff will be interviewed and asked to provide faecal specimens.

Having identified cases, the causative agent, the outbreak location, and the cause of the outbreak (by interviews and site investigation), the officer will attempt to trace the source, i.e. what brought the causative agent into the food premises or where the agent first entered the food chain, for example, the cow on the farm.

The role of the supervisor

If a supervisor suspects the business may have been responsible for a food poisoning outbreak, he/she should advise the manager, who will probably require any further food sales to be suspended, if the outbreak is very recent, until the allegation has been investigated. Any staff with boils or septic cuts or who have recently suffered from diarrhoea or vomiting, even if they are now symptom-free, should be sent to the doctor and not resume food-handling duties until medical clearance has been obtained.

Checks should be made to ensure that no other similar complaints have been received. Supervisors may be able to obtain invaluable information on the history of the suspect foods from delivery to service. In the case of retail or manufacturing, recall procedures for suspect food may need implementing.

SUPERVISING FOOD SAFETY (LEVEL 3) **Supervisory management**

Supervisors will be able to assist in the provision of necessary information for the environmental health practitioner/officer. Records provided by management may be slightly out of date because of last minute changes and the supervisor will need to check the accuracy, especially of menus, supplier lists, delivery records, staff work and sickness records, HACCP and methods of preparation. Other records that will be required include:

- temperature control (cooking and storage);
- training;
- pest control;
- cleaning schedules;
- complaint records, audit records; and
- details of customers.

Supervisors will also be given the task of ensuring the premises are thoroughly cleaned and disinfected once the officer is satisfied that they are capable of producing safe food. In addition any recommendations from the officer on preventing future outbreaks will need to be implemented.

The role of the consultant in communicable disease control (CCDC)

CCDCs are public health doctors employed by the health authorities and who work for local authorities. They are responsible for controlling public health diseases, including food poisoning, and usually chair the outbreak control team. In addition to their medical skills, they often provide the epidemiological expertise and give advice on controlling infection and treatment required. They rarely get involved in enforcement matters or the inspection of premises.

The Health Protection Agency (HPA)/Health Protection Scotland (HPS)

The HPA is a national organization for England and Wales, created on 1st April 2003 to protect people's health by minimizing risks from infectious diseases, poisons, chemicals and biological and radiation hazards. The HPA incorporates several organizations including, the Public Health Laboratory Service, the Communicable Disease Surveillance Centre, the Central Public Health Laboratory and NHS public health staff responsible for infectious disease control. Health Protection Scotland is the equivalent organization responsible for Scotland.

The HPA/HPS is responsible for:

- advising the Government on public health matters;
- delivering services to protect public health;
- providing impartial advice and information to professionals and the public;
- providing a rapid response to health protection emergencies; and
- improving knowledge of health protection through research, development, education and training.

The HPA provides surveillance and assists in the control of foodborne illness. It provides expertise and its laboratories are involved with testing food/water samples and faecal specimens.

HACCP (HAZARD ANALYSIS CRITICAL CONTROL POINT)

Food Safety Management and HACCP

Food business operators have a legal responsibility to implement a food safety management system based on the principles of HACCP (hazard analysis critical control point).

HACCP was developed in the 1960s by the Pillsbury Company and NASA to guarantee the safety of food intended for astronauts. HACCP shifts the emphasis of control from end-product testing and inspection to identifying hazards and risks and eliminating them prior to or during production. HACCP systems prioritize controls so that resources are concentrated on the points critical to food safety, for example, cooking, cooling and storage of high-risk food.

Terminology associated with HACCP

Codex Alimentarius: A collection of internationally adopted food standards and guidelines intended to protect the health of consumers and to ensure fair practices in food trade. (Produced by the Codex Alimentarius Commission of the Food and Agriculture Organisation of the United Nations and the World Health Organisation.)

Control measures: Actions or activities required to prevent or eliminate a food safety hazard or reduce it to an acceptable level.

Corrective action: The action to be taken when results of monitoring at a CCP indicate loss of control, i.e. a critical limit is breached.

Critical control point: A step in the process where control can be applied and is essential to prevent or eliminate a food safety hazard or reduce it to an acceptable level.

Critical limit: A monitored criterion which separates the acceptable from the unacceptable.

Decision tree: A sequence of questions to determine if a step in the process is a critical control point.

Deviation: Failure to meet a critical limit.

Flow diagram: A systematic representation of the sequence of steps or operations involved with a particular food item or process, usually from receipt of raw materials to consumer.

Food safety management system: The policies, procedures, practices, controls and documentation that ensure the food sold by a food business is safe to eat and free from contaminants.

HACCP (hazard analysis critical control point): A food safety management system which identifies, evaluates and controls hazards which are significant for food safety.

HACCP team: A group of people with appropriate expertise who develop and implement a HACCP system.

Hazard: A biological, chemical or physical agent in, or condition of, food with the potential to cause harm (an adverse health effect) to the consumer. (NB most biological hazards are microbiological.)

Hazard analysis (Codex Alimentarius): The process of collecting and evaluating information on hazards and conditions leading to their presence to decide which are significant for food safety and therefore should be addressed in the HACCP plan.

Monitoring: The planned observations or measurements of control parameters to confirm that the process is under control, and that critical limits are not exceeded.

Prerequisite programmes: The good hygiene practices that a food business must have in place before implementing HACCP to enable the HACCP plan to concentrate on the most significant hazards.

Risk: The likelihood of a hazard occurring in food.

Target level: Control criterion that is more stringent than the critical limit, and which can be used to reduce the risk of a deviation.

Tolerance: The specified degree of latitude for a control measure, which, if exceeded, requires immediate corrective action.

Validation: Obtaining evidence that elements of the HACCP plan are effective, especially the critical control points and critical limits.

Verification: The application of methods, procedures and tests, and other evaluations, in addition to the monitoring, to determine compliance with the HACCP plan. (Includes prerequisite programmes.)

Advantages of HACCP

- it's proactive - remedial action is taken before serious problems occur;
- cost-effective as resources targetted to where they are most needed;
- complies with legal requirements;
- reduces risk of food poisoning and food complaints (brand protection);
- demonstrates management commitment to food safety, part of a hygiene culture; and
- useful to demonstrate due diligence.

The Codex Alimentarius 7 Principles of HACCP

HACCP, as defined by Codex Alimentarius, is a food safety management system based on the following seven principles:

- conduct a hazard analysis. Prepare a flow diagram, identify the hazards and specify the control measures;
- determine the critical control points;
- establish critical limits;
- establish a system to monitor control of each CCP;
- establish corrective actions when monitoring indicates a particular CCP is not under control;
- establish procedures for verification to confirm that the HACCP system is working effectively; and
- establish documentation and records concerning all procedures appropriate to these principles and their application.

Prerequisite programmes for HACCP

Prior to the implementation of an effective HACCP system, a business must be operating in accordance with good hygiene practice or, in the case of factories, good manufacturing practice, and comply with all relevant food safety legislation. Management must be committed to the introduction of HACCP and provide adequate resources and suitable facilities. Prerequisite programmes should include:

- approved suppliers;
- premises and equipment well designed, constructed and maintained. Equipment should be calibrated. Product should flow from the delivery of raw ingredients to the production of finished products, without there being a risk of cross-contamination;
- water and ice used in food production must be potable;
- staff must be trained commensurate with their work activities; they should have high standards of personal hygiene, especially in relation to handwashing. A health and exclusion policy should exist to screen new employees and ensure that food handlers with diarrhoea and/or vomiting do not handle food until they are symptom-free for at least 48 hours and, when they return to work, they can be relied on to thoroughly wash their hands after using the toilet;
- effective planned cleaning and disinfection and the use of cleaning schedules for monitoring purposes;
- integrated pest management;
- effective waste management;
- thorough washing and disinfecting of all ready-to-eat fruit and salad vegetables;
- stock rotation; and
- labelling, traceability and recall procedures.

Good hygiene practices prevent some microbiological contaminants and the majority of physical and chemical contaminants that could occur in catering and retailing operations.

The implementation of HACCP (12 logical steps)
1. Assemble and train the HACCP team

The HACCP team must be proportionate to the size, risk and complexity of the business. The team must be aware of the hazards and controls associated with the production of food. In small businesses, one person may be the sole team member, although external consultants may also assist.

2. Describe the products or processes

A detailed description of each product will be required in manufacturing.

However, in catering or retailing it is more likely that the processes will be used as a basis for the flow diagrams. For example, perishable raw food which is cooked and served hot or, high-risk food which is served cold.

3. Identify intended users
Especially vulnerable groups such as babies, the elderly, pregnant women, ill people, those who suffer allergic reactions and those with immune deficiency.

4. Construct a flow diagram
A flow diagram is a systematic representation of the sequence of steps involved with a particular food item or process, usually from purchase of raw materials to the consumer.

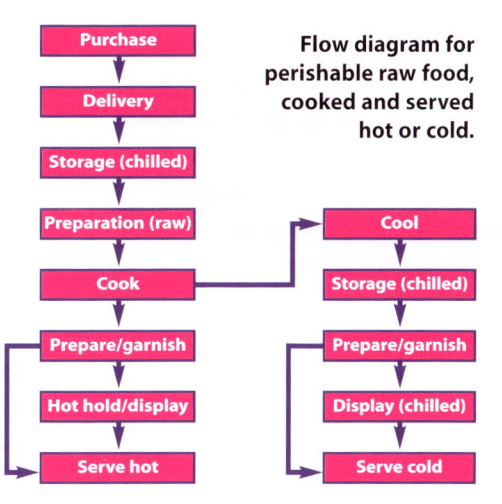

Flow diagram for perishable raw food, cooked and served hot or cold.

Purchase → Delivery → Storage (chilled) → Preparation (raw) → Cook → Prepare/garnish → Hot hold/display → Serve hot

Cook → Cool → Storage (chilled) → Prepare/garnish → Display (chilled) → Serve cold

5. Validate the flow diagram
This involves ensuring that your theoretical flow diagram accurately reflects what happens in practice.

6. Conduct a hazard analysis (Principle 1)
Hazard analysis involves:
- identifying the hazards (what could go wrong?) that may affect the process;
- identifying the steps at which the hazards are likely to occur (critical steps);
- deciding which hazards are significant, i.e. their elimination or reduction to acceptable levels is essential to the production of safe food; and
- determining the measures necessary to control the hazards (measures to prevent things going wrong).

Food safety hazards
Food safety hazards are biological, chemical or physical contaminants with the potential to cause harm to the person who consumes the contaminated food. The commonest biological hazards are microbiological.

Biological hazards include bacteria or their toxins, viruses, moulds and parasites that may cause foodborne illness. They involve:
- the contamination of ready-to-eat food by sufficient numbers of pathogens to cause illness;
- the multiplication of micro-organisms; and
- the survival of micro-organisms, for example, as a result of undercooking.

Poor temperature control or prolonged time at ambient temperature could result in any food poisoning bacteria multiplying to large numbers. A failure to cook thoroughly could result in the survival of some food poisoning bacteria.

Chemical hazards include poisonous foods such as toadstools, pesticides, cleaning chemicals and excess additives that can poison people.

Allergenic hazards (often dealt with as chemical hazards).

Physical hazards (foreign bodies) include glass, sharp metal objects and stones that may result in cuts to the mouth, broken teeth, choking and internal injury. Burning is also a physical hazard.

Physical or chemical hazards could occur at any stage in the process and it is unlikely that their removal will be guaranteed at a later stage.

Control measures

Control measures are the actions required to prevent or eliminate a food safety hazard or reduce it to an acceptable level, for example, cooking food to kill bacteria or keeping food cold in a refrigerator to stop the multiplication of bacteria. Control measures for physical contaminants include the use of metal detectors and filters and strict rules about the storage and use of chemicals.

7. Determine the critical control points (CCPs) (Principle 2)

These are steps in the process where control measures must be used to prevent food poisoning, injury or harm to the customer.

CCPs are identified by using judgement and expertise. Cooking, or processing, cooling and cold or hot storage (of high-risk foods) are usually CCPs.

8. Establish critical limits for each CCP (Principle 3)

Critical limits are values which are set for control measures to ensure the food is safe, for example, cooking to a centre temperature of 75°C, hot holding of food above 63°C or refrigerating food below 8°C. Critical limits should be unambiguous and measurable. If a critical limit is breached, for example, if refrigerated food is above 8°C for more than 4 hours, the food should be thrown away. To avoid throwing food away and to allow remedial action to be taken before a critical limit is breached it is best to set a target level, for example, store food below 5°C or cook food to 78°C. If the target level is breached, for example, the food in the refrigerator is 7°C, the thermostat can be turned down to reduce the temperature before the critical limit is breached.

Critical limits include time, temperature, size, weight and appearance/colour. Objective and measurable parameters are preferable.

9. Monitoring (checking) of control measures at each CCP (Principle 4)

Monitoring is essential to confirm that the process is under control and critical limits are not exceeded. Monitoring also ensures:
- expected standards are being achieved;
- a due-diligence defence will be assisted; and
- complaints are minimized and commitment and motivation of staff are improved.

Monitoring methods include organoleptic assessment, observation, supervision, measuring temperatures/time/weight etc., checking records, and competency.

Monitoring systems should state **WHAT** the critical limits and target levels are; **HOW** the monitoring should be undertaken; **WHERE** the monitoring should be undertaken; **WHEN** the monitoring should be undertaken; and **WHO** is responsible for monitoring. The frequency of monitoring must be cost-effective and sufficient to ensure that the hazards are controlled. Critical limits may dictate frequency to avoid wasting food, for example, if the critical limit for refrigerated food is 8ºC for 4 hours then the temperature should be measured at least every four hours.

Organoleptic assessment of food

The appearance, smell, texture, taste and other physical characteristics of food are valuable for obtaining a rapid assessment of food standards (quality, taint and spoilage). However, food contaminated by pathogenic bacteria may appear in all respects fit to eat and suspect food should not be tasted. Specific indicators include:

- **Smell** – good food should smell fresh, pleasant and natural. Unusual, stale, musty or rancid smells should invite suspicions. Chemical smells may indicate chemical contamination. Ammonia smells in some fish are an early sign of decomposition;
- **Taste** – unusual bitterness or sweetness, a soapy taste or any untypical flavour may indicate unfitness;
- **Appearance** – food should be visibly free from signs of spoilage, fungal growth, slime, darkening or other change in colour, untypical wetness and mechanical damage. Absence of foreign objects and dirt in finished goods, including pests, pest debris and parasites, is important. Meat, poultry and fish should be free from signs of disease or other pathological conditions. In frozen food, excessive ice can be an indicator of mishandling, as can large ice crystals within the texture; loose foods such as peas should not be welded together. A final judgement of frozen food can only be made after defrosting;
- **Sound** – many packed foods, especially canned goods, emit a characteristic sound on being tapped or shaken. Any such food or pack emitting an untypical sound is suspect;
- **Texture** – unusual softness, hardness, brittleness or change in texture may be indicative of unfitness. Meat, fish and certain other products, such as cheese, should display a springy texture. Light pressure from a finger that causes an indentation to remain can be significant.

Bacteriological monitoring

Bacteriological monitoring can be used to assist the verification of HACCP but is also commonly used in manufacturing premises to:

- build up a profile of product quality;
- indicate trends in product quality;
- ascertain whether handling techniques are satisfactory;

- indicate product safety and the absence of specific organisms or pathogens;
- determine effectiveness of cleaning and disinfection;
- determine effectiveness of processing;
- confirm that legal standards or customer's specifications are being met.

However, bacteriological monitoring has the following disadvantages:
- it is usually retrospective and cannot be used to verify product safety where there is a short time between production and consumption, for example, in conventional catering or for products with short shelf lives;
- it is relatively expensive;
- considerable expertise may be needed to interpret results and relate them to product age;
- the non-uniform distribution of bacteria in foods and the effect of different laboratory techniques and sampling methods significantly affect the results;
- the operation is being controlled by a laboratory technician who may be remote from the food production;
- only a limited number of samples can be taken;
- not all hazards are identified; and
- only a small section of the workforce assumes responsibility for product safety.

Monitoring of food handlers

Monitoring of food handlers by supervisors is essential to identify failures in personal hygiene or hygiene practices and to identify training needs. Monitoring can involve observation, for example, to ensure staff wash their hands properly when entering the food room and to ensure protective clothing is clean, put on and worn correctly. More formal monitoring can involve bacteriological swabbing of fingers, competency testing and annual medical checks by medical staff to reinforce rules relating to illness.

10. Establish corrective actions (Principle 5)

Corrective action is the action taken when a critical limit is breached. It involves two distinct parts: firstly, dealing with the affected product (for example, destroying the product or reducing the shelf life), and secondly, bringing the process back under control.

Corrective action would be necessary if, for example, the food in the refrigerator was at too high a temperature. The action taken may be to turn the thermostat down and to destroy the food if it had been above 8°C for more than four hours. In the event of a metal nut being found in someone's meal, sales of any suspect food should be stopped immediately. A full investigation would be required to ascertain if there was a possible source for the nut in the kitchen. If not, the supplier must be notified.

Staff should be asked to be particularly vigilant for any further problems. If a used blue plaster is found in the mixing bowl, the contents of the bowl should be discarded. The person responsible, if on-site, should be traced so that an additional larger plaster can be provided. Staff should be reminded of the need to ensure plasters don't become detached and that finger cots may be needed.

If a food handler uses a bowl for mixing a high-risk food after use for mixing raw egg he/she should be instructed on the risks and advised of the consequences if it is done again. The high-risk food food should be discarded and the bowl cleaned and disinfected.

Procedures for corrective action should specify: the action to be taken; who should take the action; who should be notified; whether or not production/sales should continue; whether products should be recalled; how the product should be dealt with; and who can authorize the re-start of production or sales.

Manufacturers, wholesalers and retailers should ensure that all products are clearly labelled and traceable in the event of a recall being necessary.

11. Establish verification procedures (proof that the HACCP system is working) (Principle 6)

Verification involves the use of methods, procedures and tests, in addition to those used in monitoring, to demonstrate that the HACCP system is working effectively. Auditing the HACCP system to ensure all hazards and CCPs have been identified and controls and monitoring remain effective is the most common verification technique. All scientific data on which the system is based can be re-examined to ensure it is still applicable. Monitoring records, deviations and complaints can be examined. Part of verification is validation i.e. obtaining evidence that elements of the HACCP plan are effective, especially the critical control points and critical limits.

Does the control eliminate the hazard, for example, prove that the cooking or processing temperature and time is adequate to make the food safe?

The HACCP plan should be reviewed periodically and particularly if:
- a justified complaint is received or illness occurs;
- raw materials change e.g. fresh chicken instead of frozen;
- the recipe changes, e.g. salt is removed;
- equipment changes, e.g. a blast chiller is introduced; and
- packaging or distribution changes, e.g. refrigerated transport is utilized.

Persons involved in verification may include, external consultants, persons responsible for the HACCP system, staff involved with controls/monitoring, supervisors/managers and enforcement officers.

12. Establish documentation and record-keeping (Principle 7)

The amount and type of paperwork required to support HACCP systems should be proportionate to the size and type of food business and the risks involved with the process. Documentation is useful to demonstrate that food safety is being managed and, provided records are completed accurately at the appropriate time, they are useful to support a due-diligence defence if this is required in court.

SUPERVISING FOOD SAFETY (LEVEL 3) Supervisory management

The documentation to support the HACCP study may include:
- the HACCP plan;
- a floor plan;
- the prerequisite programmes;
- audit reports;
- the approved supplier list;
- monitoring records (such as: deliveries, training records, refrigerator and freezer temperatures, cleaning schedules, stock rotation, pest control and exclusion records). All monitoring records should be signed and dated. (Paperwork will be reduced if records are only kept for critical control points). Obsolete instructions/documentation must always be withdrawn.

TEMPERATURE CHECK - COLD
Records for Week Commencing ..../.........../...........

Fridge number/place	Saturday am	Saturday pm	Sunday am	Sunday pm	Monday am	Monday pm	Tuesday am	Tuesday pm	Wednesday am	Wednesday pm	Thursday am	Thursday pm	Friday am	Friday pm
Fridge one														
Fridge two														
Fridge three														
Fridge four														
Fridge five														
Supervisor's initials (am & pm)														

For any situations above 8°C, record action taken

Signature: .... Date ....

The HACCP plan may include:
- details of the HACCP team;
- the scope and terms of reference;
- the product or process description;
- flow diagrams;
- consumers;
- hazard analysis and CCP determination;
- critical limits and targets, deviations and corrective actions; and
- validation, verification and review procedures.

Some of this documentation will be itemised on the HACCP control chart.

SUPERVISING FOOD SAFETY (LEVEL 3) Supervisory management

The following table is known as a HACCP control chart and includes examples of typical hazards, control measures, monitoring and corrective actions.

STEP	Hazards	Control measures & critical limits	Monitoring	Corrective action*
PURCHASE	Contamination with harmful bacteria, toxic chemicals or foreign bodies.	Use only reputable suppliers. Select least hazardous ingredients. Product specification. Purchase branded products.	Ensure supplier has effective HACCP system and good hygiene practices. Obtain HACCP documentation. Inspect supplier's business. Utilize customer references.	Revisit/audit supplier's premises. Review product specification. Warn supplier. Change supplier.
DELIVERY & UNLOADING	Contamination with harmful bacteria, toxic chemicals or foreign bodies. Multiplication of food poisoning bacteria.	Food covered/protected or in suitable containers. Deboxing area. Use only approved suppliers. Date codes/labels. Specific delivery requirements. (NOT with toxic chemicals.) Chilled food below 5ºC. (Critical limit 8ºC.) Frozen food below –18ºC. Move to storage within 15 minutes of unloading.	Observation (visual and sensory checks.) Condition of packaging/food. Conditions of vehicle/driver. Supplier on the approved supplier list. Food is within date code. Food is delivered in accordance with specification. Temperature of food using calibrated probe thermometer. Time to move to storage.	Change supplier. Review/reissue product specification/instructions. Refuse delivery. Return stock. Inform chef or manager. Review systems/training.
CHILLED STORAGE	Contamination with harmful bacteria, toxic chemicals or foreign bodies. Multiplication of food poisoning bacteria.	Food covered/protected. Segregation of raw and high-risk food. Use disinfected temperature probe. Food not stored in open cans. Load food correctly. Chilled food below 5ºC. (Critical limit >8ºC for 2 hours.) Don't overload refrigerator. Good stock rotation procedures. Date codes/labels.	Observation. Condition of food. Condition of packaging. Air temperature. In-between pack temperature. Temperature of food. Time above 8ºC. Door seals. Food is within date code.	Inform chef or manager. Discard unfit or out-of-date food. Review systems/training. Adjust thermostat. Reorganize refrigerator in order to allow good air circulation. Call out refrigerator engineer. Repair/replace fridge. Implement contingency plan.
FROZEN STORAGE	Multiplication of food poisoning bacteria.	Food frozen below –18ºC.	Observation. Air temperature. In-between pack temperature. Temperature of food.	Inform chef or manager. Discard unfit or out-of-date food. Review systems/training. Adjust thermostat. Call out refrigerator engineer. Replace freezer. Implement contingency plan.
DRY STORAGE	Contamination with harmful bacteria, toxic chemicals or foreign bodies. Multiplication of food poisoning bacteria.	Food covered/protected or in suitable containers. Care in handling. Maintain in a cool, dry condition. Food within date code. Good stock rotation.	Observation. Condition of packaging. Condition of food. Condition of canned goods. Housekeeping.	Inform chef or manager. Discard unsatisfactory food. Review systems/training. Building maintenance to remove dampness. Store out of direct sunlight.

SUPERVISING FOOD SAFETY (LEVEL 3) Supervisory management

STEP	Hazards	Control measures & critical limits	Monitoring	Corrective action*
PREPARATION	Contamination with harmful bacteria, toxic chemicals or foreign bodies.	Separation of raw and high-risk food. Use separate equipment. Colour coding. Organisation/workflow. Disposable cloths/paper roll. Minimize handling of ready-to-eat food where practical. Thoroughly wash all ready-to-eat produce and garnishes. Don't top up sauces. Exclude staff with food poisoning symptoms.	Observation. Staff sickness record and exclusions.	Inform chef or manager. Discard contaminated food. Review systems/training.
	Multiplication of food poisoning bacteria.	Maximum time at room temperature 30 minutes. (Critical limit 2 hours) Pre-cool salad sandwich ingredients. Minimize quantities prepared. Portion control.	Temperature of food. Time at room temperature.	Discard high-risk food left at room temperature for >2 hours. Reduce quantities prepared.
THAWING	Multiplication of food poisoning bacteria.	High-risk food should be thawed in a refrigerator. Use thawed food within 24 hours. (Label)	Observation. Temperature of food.	Inform chef or manager. Discard food which has thawed and then been left at room temperature for >2 hours.
	Contamination with harmful bacteria, toxic chemicals or foreign bodies.	High-risk and raw food should not be thawed in the same area. Raw food should not be thawed in areas used for cooling cooked food.		Discard contaminated food. Review systems/training.
	Survival of food poisoning bacteria (during cooking).	Raw frozen food must be completely thawed, especially poultry. (Critical limit - absence of ice.)	Temperature/visual and physical checks.	Continue thawing. Allow longer thawing time in future.
COOKING/REHEATING	Survival of harmful bacteria/spores and/or toxins.	Cook thoroughly to 78ºC. Critical limit 75ºC (or equivalent time and temperature.) Boil liquids. Don't reheat more than once. Contingency plans. Cook/reheat just before eating. Follow microwave procedures. Follow instruction on packaging. Stir liquids. Ensure frozen meat and poultry are completely thawed prior to cooking.	Core temperature of food. Observation.	Inform chef or manager. Extend cooking time until core temperature of 78ºC is reached. Allow longer cooking time/higher oven temperature in future. Carry out cooking trials. Discard simmering high-risk liquids that have not been stirred for more than 2 hours. If less than 2 hours, stir liquid and bring to boil. Call out engineer. Implement contingency plan. Review systems/training.
	Contamination with toxic chemicals or foreign bodies.	Avoid copper and aluminium for acid food. Protect from contamination.		Repair/replace unsatisfactory equipment and pans.

SUPERVISING FOOD SAFETY (LEVEL 3) Supervisory management

STEP	Hazards	Control measures & critical limits	Monitoring	Corrective action*
COOLING	Contamination with harmful bacteria, toxic chemicals or foreign bodies.	Separation of raw and high-risk food. Protect from contamination.	Observation. Time to cool. Temperature of food.	Inform chef or manager. Discard contaminated food. Review systems/training. Discard food if not cooled and refrigerated within critical time. Call out engineer. Repair/replace blast chiller.
	Multiplication of food poisoning bacteria, formation of toxins and/or germination of spores.	Rapid cooling (blast chiller) and refrigeration. Minimize weight/thickness of joints, e.g. 2 kgs. Cool liquids in clean, shallow trays (maximum depth 25mm.) Blast chiller (90 minutes.) 63°C to 20°C in <2 hours. (Critical limit in >3 hours.) 20°C to 7°C in <4 hours. (Critical limit in >5hours.)		
HOT HOLDING	Contamination with harmful bacteria, toxic chemicals or foreign bodies.	Protect from contamination. Sneeze guards etc. if hot holding for service. Use disinfected temperature probe.	Observation.	Inform chef or manager. Discard contaminated food. Review systems/training.
	Multiplication of food poisoning bacteria, formation of toxins and/or germination of spores.	Maintain at the correct temperature (minimum 63°C). (Critical limit <63°C for 2 hours.) Minimize quantities. Preheat hot holding equipment. Contingency plans.	Time and temperature of food.	Adjust thermostat. Discard any food that has been maintained at below 63°C for more than 2 hours. Call out engineer. Repair/replace equipment. Implement contingency plan.
COLD DISPLAY	Contamination with harmful bacteria, toxic chemicals or foreign bodies.	Food covered/protected, e.g. sneeze screens. Segregation of raw and high-risk food. Use disinfected temperature probe. Minimize handling, use long handled tongs/serving utensils.	Observation.	Inform chef or manager. Discard contaminated food. Review systems/training.
	Multiplication of food poisoning bacteria.	Food stored below 5°C. (Critical limit >8°C for 4 hours.) Good stock rotation.	Air temperature. In-between pack temperature. Temperature of food. Time above 8°C. Food is within date code.	Adjust thermostat. Discard any food >8°C for 4 hours. Call out engineer. Implement contingency plan.
SERVICE	Contamination with harmful bacteria, toxic chemicals or foreign bodies.	Protect from contamination. Minimize handling. Separate staff handling raw and high-risk food. Colour coding. Handwashing between handling soiled crockery and/or cutlery.	Observation.	Inform chef or manager. Discard contaminated food. Review systems/training.
	Multiplication of food poisoning bacteria.	Minimize time high-risk food is at room temperature. Serve within 15 minutes of cooking, hot holding, chill storage or preparation.		

† Frequency of checks and person responsible should be included. Monitoring records will usually be needed at most steps.
* Person responsible for corrective action should be included.

N.B. Effective supervision, instruction and competency training are controls at each step. High standards of personal hygiene, integrated pest management, effective cleaning and disinfection and maintenance are prerequisites to the implementation of HACCP and are not included within the HACCP control chart. However, they are controls that apply at most steps. Chemical and physical hazards are mainly dealt with through the prerequisite programmes.

Safer food better business (SFBB)
SFBB is a food safety management system developed by the Food Standards Agency (England). It is divided into two parts. The first part provides safe methods and the second part is concerned with monitoring and verification. The safe methods relate to cross-contamination (including personal hygiene), cleaning (including handwashing), chilling and cooking. There is also a section on management which provides guidance on opening and closing checks, proving methods are safe, a safe method completion record, training and supervision, stock control and selecting suppliers and contractors.

Opening checks include: checking fridges and equipment; staff fitness; cleanliness of surfaces; and that adequate cleaning materials are provided.
Closing checks include: no food left out; out-of-date food discarded, all dirty cloths replaced; and all waste removed.

The monitoring section includes a cleaning schedule, a suppliers' list, staff training records, a diary to record daily events, and a four weekly review to support verification. The safe method sheets are based on good catering practice. They identify generic hazards and critical control points and describe how to prepare safe food. Safe method sheets must be completed by each business to ensure that the pack is customized to reflect the critical control points specific to their operation. The business must complete all safe methods relative to their operation and, if necessary, develop their own safe methods for menu items or practices not included in the pack. The manager must sign the diary every day to confirm that all safety checks were carried out and that the safe methods were followed. If something different happens or something went wrong, this should be recorded in the diary, together with the corrective action that was taken to make the food safe to eat. Verification that the system remains effective is achieved by the four weekly audit, inspections by environmental health practitioners/officers and the validation (prove-it) part of the management section. SFBB does not require the daily use of a probe thermometer. However, the correct use of a probe thermometer, for example, to check deliveries and storage temperatures, to confirm cooking temperatures and to confirm that food on display is kept below 8ºC or above 63ºC will enhance the safety of the operation.

CookSafe Food Safety Assurance System
CookSafe is a food safety management system developed by the Food Standards Agency (Scotland). It is divided into five sections. The first section provides key definitions and details of how HACCP works. This is followed by advice on constructing a flow diagram specific to your operation and based on the template provided. The third section provides generic HACCP charts for most process steps from purchase to service. Charts include details of hazards, control measures and critical limits, monitoring and recording and corrective action. Charts will need to be completed relevant to the process steps of your specific business and this requires using the fourth section of the manual, the house rules. The house rules include advice on both prerequisite programmes, such as personal hygiene and cleaning as well as guidance on critical limits, and monitoring, for example temperature control. Using the template provided you are expected to draw up your own house rules and complete the HACCP charts. The final section of CookSafe provides guidance on recording and includes photocopiable monitoring forms, for example, temperature monitoring records and cleaning schedules.

12 Food safety legislation

The law is a complex subject and most acts and regulations affecting the food industry are difficult to interpret. However, ignorance of the law is no defence in the event of a prosecution and supervisors must make a special effort to become conversant with legislation which affects their work.

This chapter includes an outline of the most important legislation relating to food and food hygiene in Scotland, England and Wales; Northern Ireland has its own legislation, although any differences are usually minor. Should information or advice be required regarding the interpretation of a particular section, or the current legislation applicable, the local environmental health practitioner/officer or a solicitor should be consulted.

Legislation consists of: Acts of Parliament which are concerned with principles of legislation; regulations and orders which normally deal with specific premises or commodities in much greater detail than acts; and local acts or by-laws which are made or adopted by local authorities and are legally binding only within the area of the particular authority.

In the event of any legal query, it is always best to consult someone conversant with the specifics of both the legal system and the subject matter in question.

Acts and regulations applicable to the food industry are concerned with:
- preventing the production or sale of injurious, unsafe or unfit food;
- preventing the contamination of food and food equipment;
- the hygiene of food premises, equipment and personnel (including training);
- hygiene practices, including temperature control and the control and monitoring of hazards at points which are critical to food safety;
- the provision of sanitary accommodation, water supplies and washing facilities;
- the control of food poisoning;
- the importation of food;
- the composition and labelling of food; and
- the registration and licensing of food premises and vehicles.

The European Union

Most legislation relating to food safety is now imposed by the European Union in the form of regulations or directives. EU regulations apply without modification whereas directives require the member states to introduce their own legislation to achieve the objectives of the directive.

Regulation (EC) No 852/2004 on the hygiene of foodstuffs
Article 5.
Food business operators must implement a food safety management system based on the following HACCP principles:
- **(a)** identifying hazards;
- **(b)** identifying the critical control points (CCPs) at the steps at which control is essential to prevent or eliminate a hazard or to reduce it to acceptable levels;
- **(c)** establishing critical limits at CCPs which separate acceptability from unacceptability;
- **(d)** implementing effective monitoring procedures at CCPs;
- **(e)** establishing corrective actions when a CCP is out of control;
- **(f)** establishing verification procedures
- **(g)** establishing documents and records commensurate with the nature and size of the food business. (Documents must be kept up to date and retained for an appropriate period.)

The system must be reviewed if the product, process or any step is modified.

Article 6.
Food business operators must register with the competent authority (usually the local authority). Registration should be at least 28 days before opening.

Significant changes in activities must be reported to the competent authority.

Article 8.
National guides to good practice shall be developed by food business sectors in consultation with competent authorities and consumer groups.

Annex II (General hygiene requirements)
Chapter I (General requirements for food premises)
- Food premises are to be kept clean and maintained in good repair and condition.
- The design, layout, construction, siting and size of food premises are to:
    - **(a)** permit adequate maintenance, cleaning and/or disinfection, minimize airborne contamination, and provide adequate working space to allow for the hygienic performance of all operations;
    - **(b)** be such as to protect against the accumulation of dirt, contact with toxic materials, the shedding of particles into food and the formation of condensation or undesirable mould on surfaces;
    - **(c)** permit good food hygiene practices, including protection against contamination and, in particular, pest control; and
    - **(d)** where necessary provide suitable temperature controlled handling and storage conditions of sufficient capacity for maintaining foodstuffs at appropriate temperatures to be monitored and, where necessary, recorded.

- An adequate number of flush lavatories are to be available. Lavatories are not to open directly into rooms in which food is handled.
- An adequate number of washbasins are to be available, suitably located and designated for cleaning hands. Washbasins are to be provided with hot and cold running water, and materials for cleaning, hands and for hygienic drying. Where necessary, the facilities for washing food are to be separate from the handwashing facility.
- There is to be suitable and sufficient means of natural or mechanical ventilation. Mechanical air flow from a contaminated area to a clean area is to be avoided. Ventilation systems are to be so constructed as to enable filters and other parts requiring cleaning or replacement to be readily accessible.
- Sanitary conveniences are to have adequate natural or mechanical ventilation.
- Food premises are to have adequate natural and/or artificial lighting.
- Drainage facilities are to be adequate for the purpose intended. They are to be designed and constructed to avoid the risk of contamination.
- Where necessary, adequate changing facilities for personnel are to be provided.
- Cleaning agents and disinfectants are not to be stored in areas where food is handled.

Chapter II (Specific requirements in rooms where foodstuffs are prepared, treated or processed)

(1) The design and layout of the rooms are to permit good food hygiene practices, including protection against contamination between and during operations. In particular:

   (a) floor surfaces are to be maintained in a sound condition and be easy to clean and, where necessary, to disinfect. This will require the use of impervious, washable and non-toxic materials, unless the food business operators can satisfy the competent authority that other materials used are appropriate. Where appropriate, floors are to allow adequate surface drainage;

   (b) wall surfaces are to be maintained in a sound condition and be easy to clean and, where necessary to, disinfect. This will require the use of impervious, washable and non-toxic materials and require a smooth surface up to a height appropriate for the operations, unless food business operators can satisfy the competent authority that other materials used are appropriate;

   (c) ceilings and overhead fixtures are to be designed, constructed and finished so as to prevent the accumulation of dirt and to reduce condensation, the growth of undesirable moulds and the shedding of particles;

(d) windows and other openings are to be constructed to prevent the accumulation of dirt. Those which can be opened to the outside environment are, where necessary, to be fitted with insect-proof screens which can be easily removed for cleaning. Where open windows would result in contamination, windows are to remain closed and fixed during production;

(e) doors are to be easy to clean and, where necessary, to disinfect. This will require the use of smooth and non-absorbent surfaces, unless the food business operators can satisfy the competent authority that other materials used are appropriate; and

(f) surfaces (including surfaces of equipment) in areas where foods are handled and in particular those in contact with food are to be maintained in sound condition and be easy to clean and, where necessary, to disinfect. This will require the use of smooth, washable, corrosion-resistant and non-toxic materials, unless food business operators can satisfy the competent authority that other materials used are appropriate.

(2) Adequate facilities are to be provided, where necessary, for the cleaning, disinfecting and storage of working utensils and equipment. These facilities are to be constructed of corrosion-resistant materials, be easy to clean and have an adequate supply of hot and cold water.

(3) Adequate provision is to be made, where necessary, for washing food. Every sink or other such facility provided for the washing of food is to have an adequate supply of hot and/or cold potable water, and be kept clean, and where necessary, disinfected.

Chapter III (Requirements for market stalls or mobile sales vehicles, premises used primarily as a private dwelling house, premises used occasionally for catering purposes and vending machines)

Premises and vending machines are, so far as is reasonably practicable, to be sited, designed, constructed, kept clean and maintained in good repair and condition as to avoid the risk of contamination, in particular by animals and pests.

Surfaces in contact with food are to be in a sound condition and be easy to clean and, where necessary, to disinfect.

Where necessary, there are to be facilities to maintain adequate personal hygiene and for the cleaning and, where necessary, disinfecting of working utensils and equipment.

Adequate facilities and/or arrangements for maintaining and monitoring suitable food temperature conditions are to be available.

Foodstuffs are to be placed so as to avoid the risk of contamination.

Chapter IV (Transport)

Conveyances and/or containers used for transporting foodstuffs are to be kept clean and maintained in good repair and condition to protect foodstuffs from contamination, and are, where necessary, to be designed and constructed to permit adequate cleaning and/or disinfection.

Chapter V (Equipment requirements)

All articles, fittings and equipment with which food comes into contact are to:

- **(a)** be effectively cleaned and, where necessary, disinfected. Cleaning and disinfection are to take place at a frequency sufficient to avoid any risk of contamination;

- **(b & c)** be so constructed, be of such materials and be kept in such good order, repair and condition as to minimise any risk of contamination and to enable them to be kept clean and, where necessary, to be disinfected; and

- **(d)** be installed in such a manner as to allow adequate cleaning of the equipment and the surrounding area. Where necessary, equipment is to be fitted with any appropriate control device to guarantee fulfilment of this regulation's objective.

Chapter VI (Food waste)

Food waste, non-edible by-products and other refuse are to be removed from food rooms as quickly as possible, so as to avoid their accumulation.

Waste is to be deposited in closable containers (unless the competent authority agree otherwise). Containers are to be of an appropriate construction, kept in sound condition, be easy to clean and, where necessary, to disinfect.

Adequate provision is to be made for the storage of waste. Refuse stores are to be kept clean and free of animals and pests.

All waste is to be eliminated in a hygienic and environmentally friendly way and is not to constitute a direct or indirect source of contamination.

Chapter VII (Water supply)

An adequate supply of potable water must be provided and used to ensure foodstuffs are not contaminated. Ice is to be made from potable water, if it could contaminate the food. It is to be made, handled and stored to protect it from contamination.

Where heat treatment is applied to foodstuffs in hermetically sealed containers it is to be ensured that water used to cool the containers after heat treatment is not a source of contamination for the foodstuff.

Chapter VIII (Personal hygiene)

Persons working in food handling areas are to maintain a high degree of personal cleanliness and wear suitable, clean and, where necessary, protective clothing.

No person suffering from, or being a carrier of, a foodborne disease, or afflicted with infected wounds, skin infections, sores or diarrhoea is to be permitted to handle food or enter any food handling area in any capacity if there is a likelihood of direct or indirect contamination. Any person so affected and employed in a food business and who is likely to come into contact with food is to report immediately the illness or symptoms, and if possible their causes, to the food business operator.

Chapter IX (Provisions applicable to foodstuffs)

Contaminated or decomposed raw materials must be rejected unless normal sorting and hygienic preparation will ensure their fitness for human consumption.

All food must be protected against contamination during handling, storage, packaging, display and distribution.

Effective pest control procedures must be implemented.

Food likely to support the reproduction of pathogenic micro-organisms or the formation of toxins is not to be kept at temperatures that might result in a risk to health. Food businesses manufacturing, handling and wrapping processed foodstuffs are to have suitable rooms, large enough to separate the storage of raw materials from processed material, and sufficient separate refrigerated storage.

Where foodstuffs are to be held or served at chilled temperatures they are to be cooled as quickly as possible following the heat-processing stage, or final preparation stage if no heat process is applied, to a temperature which does not result in a risk to health.

The thawing of foodstuffs is to be undertaken in such a way as to minimise the risk of growth of pathogenic micro-organisms or the formation of toxins in the foods.

Hazardous and/or inedible substances, including animal feed, are to be adequately labelled and stored in separate and secure containers.

Chapter X (Provisions applicable to the wrapping and packaging of foodstuffs)

Materials used for wrapping are not to be a source of contamination. They must be stored in such a manner that they are not exposed to a risk of contamination.

Wrapping and packaging operations are to avoid contamination of the products. The integrity and cleanliness of cans and glass jars are to be assured.

Reusable wrapping and packaging material are to be easy to clean and, where necessary, to disinfect.

Chapter XI (Heat treatment)

Heat treatment of food in hermetically sealed containers should conform to an internationally recognised standard (for example, pasteurization, ultra high temperature or sterilization). Every part of the product should achieve a given temperature for a given period of time.

SUPERVISING FOOD SAFETY (LEVEL 3) **Food safety legislation**

Chapter XII (Training)
Food business operators are to ensure:
(1) that food handlers are supervised and instructed and/or trained in food hygiene matters commensurate with their work activity; and
(2) that those responsible for the development and maintenance of the HACCP system or for the operation of relevant guides have received adequate training in the application of the HACCP principles.

The Food Hygiene (England) (Wales) (Scotland) (NI) Regulations 2006
Part 1 Preliminary

Reg 2. "Authorized officer" means any person authorized in writing by an enforcement authority to act in matters arising under the Hygiene Regulations (examples include environmental practitioner, environmental health officer, technical officer etc.)
"Hygiene Regulations" means these Regulations and Regulation (EC) 852/2004 on the hygiene of foodstuffs, Regulation (EC) 853/2004 for food of animal origin and Regulation (EC) 854/2004 for controls on products of animal origin intended for human consumption as amended by Regulation EC 882/2004 and as read with Directive 2004/41.
"Premises" includes any establishment, any place, vehicle, stall or moveable structure and any ship or aircraft.

Reg 3. Food commonly used for human consumption found on food premises shall be presumed, until the contrary is proved, to be intended for human consumption.

Part 2 Main provisions

Reg 6. An authorized officer can serve a **hygiene improvement notice** on the food business operator of a food business, for failing to comply with Hygiene Regulations. The **notice** will include the name and address of the business and must state the grounds for non-compliance, specify the contraventions and measures necessary to secure compliance, and the time (not less than 14 days) allowed. Failure to comply is an offence.

Reg 7. If a food business operator is convicted of an offence under the above regulations **and** the court is satisfied that the business, any process/treatment, the construction or condition of any premises or the use or condition of any equipment involves a risk of injury to health, they **shall** impose a **hygiene prohibition order**. A **hygiene prohibition order** can apply to the use of a process/treatment, the premises (or part thereof) or any equipment. A copy of the **hygiene prohibition order** must be conspicuously fixed on the premises and contravention of the **order** is an offence. The hygiene prohibition order ceases to have effect when the enforcement authority issues a certificate, which states that there is no longer a health risk. On application by the food business operator, the enforcement authority must determine within 14 days whether the health risk has been removed and if so satisfied, issue the certificate within three days.

The court may also impose a prohibition on the proprietor or manager participating in the management of any food business. (Only a court can lift a **hygiene prohibition order** on a food business operator.) This prohibition applies for at least six months.

Reg 8. If an authorized officer of an enforcement authority is satisfied that there is an imminent risk of injury to health, he/she may issue a **hygiene emergency prohibition notice** requiring the immediate closure of the premises. An application for a **hygiene emergency prohibition order** must then be made to the court within three days (five days in Scotland) of serving the notice, and at least one day before the date of application, the food business operator must be advised of this intention. (Saturdays, Sundays and Bank Holidays are excluded.)

The **hygiene emergency prohibition notice** and **hygiene emergency prohibition order** must be served on the food business operator and conspicuously displayed on the premises. Any contravention is an offence. A hygiene emergency prohibition notice ceases to have effect if no application for an order is made to the court. A **hygiene emergency prohibition notice/order** ceases to have effect when the enforcement authority issues a certificate, stating that there is no longer a health risk.

Compensation is payable by the enforcement authority in respect of loss suffered in complying with the **notice**, unless an application is made for a **hygiene emergency prohibition order** within three days (five days in Scotland) **and** the court is satisfied that the health risk condition was fulfilled.

The Food Law Code of Practice provides guidance on the use of hygiene improvement notices and prohibition procedures. (Details available in www.foodstandards.gov.uk)

Reg 10. Enables proceedings to be taken against another person when the offence was due to his/her act or default.

Reg 11. It is a defence for the accused to prove that he took all reasonable precautions and exercised all **due diligence** to avoid commission of the offence by himself or by a person under his control.

Part 3 Administration and enforcement

Reg 12. & 13. Empowers an authorized officer to purchase or take samples of food, food sources, contact materials or any article or substance required as evidence.

Reg 14. Empowers an authorized officer, on production of an authenticated document showing his/her authority, to enter any premises within his/her area at all reasonable hours to carry out his/her duties under the hygiene regulations. In the case of a private dwelling house, entry cannot be demanded unless 24 hours' notice has been given to the occupier. An authorized officer is also empowered to enter any business premises outside

SUPERVISING FOOD SAFETY (LEVEL 3) Food safety legislation

his/her area for the purpose of ascertaining whether or not there are any contraventions of the hygiene regulations or regulations/orders made thereunder. Warrants may be issued by a Justice of the Peace authorizing entry, by force if necessary, when entry is refused.

Authorized officers can inspect, seize and detain records, including computer records, required as evidence. Improper disclosure of information so obtained is an offence.

Reg 15. It is an offence to obstruct persons executing the provisions of the hygiene regulations, including the failure to assist or provide information (unless it incriminates them) or the furnishing of false information.

Reg 17. A person guilty of an offence under these regulations shall be liable on:
  (a) summary conviction to a fine not exceeding the statutory maximum (level 5*); or
  (b) conviction on indictment to imprisonment for up to two years and/or an unlimited fine.

The penalty for obstruction on summary conviction shall be a fine not exceeding Level 5* and/or up to three months' imprisonment.

Reg 18. Where an offence by a body corporate has been committed with the consent or connivance or due to the neglect on the part of any director, manager, secretary or similar officer, he shall also be liable to prosecution.

Reg 20. & 21. Enable aggrieved persons to appeal to the magistrates' court or the crown court.

Reg 22. Allows for appeals against hygiene improvement notices and remedial action notices.

Reg 23. Section 9 of the Food Safety Act 1990 (inspection and seizure of suspected food) applies to these regulations as regards an authorized officer of an enforcement authority.

Part 4 Miscellaneous and supplementary provisions

Reg 25. Officers of enforcement authorities are not personally liable for acts involved with the execution of the Hygiene Regulations provided they honestly believed such action was necessary.

Reg 27. When an authorized officer certifies that food has not been produced, processed or distributed in accordance with the Hygiene Regulations, it shall be treated as failing to comply with food safety requirements in accord with Section 9 of the Food Safety Act. All food within a batch shall be treated as certified until it is proved that the rest of the food was dealt with in compliance with the Hygiene Regulations.

Schedule 4 Temperature control requirements

  (1) Schedule does not apply to slaughterhouses and cutting premises or any food business operations on ships or aircraft.

*The Criminal Justice Act, 1991 provided fines for summary offences in magistrates' courts to be placed on a scale of levels 1 to 5, unless otherwise stipulated in a particular act.
Level 1 – £200   Level 2 – £500   Level 3 – £1,000   Level 4 – £2,500   Level 5 – £5,000

SUPERVISING FOOD SAFETY (LEVEL 3) Food safety legislation

Chill holding requirements
Food which supports the growth of pathogens or the formation of toxins must not be kept above 8°C unless:
- it is hot food on display;
- there is no health risk;
- it is canned or dehydrated (until opened); and
- it is raw food intended for cooking or further processing.

Chill holding tolerance periods
Food may be kept above 8°C if the manufacturer has undertaken a scientific assessment confirming there is no risk and the shelf life is not exceeded.

Food on display, or for service, may be kept above 8°C for up to four hours on a single occasion. Food may also be kept above 8°C during loading or unloading or for unavoidable reasons, such as defrosting equipment or breakdowns, provided this is consistent with food safety.

Hot holding requirements
Hot food on display must not be kept below 63°C. Food may be kept below 63°C if a scientific assessment has indicated there is no health risk.

Hot food for service or display may be kept below 63°C for up to two hours on a single occasion.

Temperature Control Requirements in Scotland
Chill holding
Food should be kept in a refrigerator or a cool ventilated place or above 63°C unless:
- **(a)** it is undergoing preparation for sale;
- **(b)** it is exposed for sale or has been sold;
- **(c)** it is being cooled under hygienic conditions as quickly as possible to a safe temperature immediately following cooking or the final processing stage; and
- **(d)** being kept at ambient temperatures poses no risk to health.

Reheating of food
Food which is to be reheated before being served for immediate consumption or exposed for sale shall be raised to a temperature of not less than 82°C, unless this would result in a deterioration in its qualities.

Raw milk
It is an offence for any person to place on the market raw milk or raw cream intended for direct human consumption.

It is a defence to prove that the raw milk or raw cream was intended for export, for example, to England, Wales, Northern Ireland or other member state or third country as long as it complies with Regulation 253/2004 and any relevant national rules.

SUPERVISING FOOD SAFETY (LEVEL 3) Food safety legislation

The Food Safety Act, 1990

As a result of the EU Hygiene Regulations and the Food Hygiene (England) (Wales) (Scotland) (NI) Regulations 2006, this Act is now primarily concerned with food standards.

Section 2. Extends the meaning of 'sale' to include food which is offered as a prize or reward or given away in connection with any entertainment for the public.

Section 3. Food, or ingredients, commonly used for human consumption are presumed, until the contrary is proved, to be intended for sale for human consumption.

Section 7. It is an offence to treat food so as to render it injurious to health with the intent that the food will be sold in that state. Regard shall be had to the cumulative effect of foods consumed over a long period.

Section 9. An authorized officer of a food authority may seize or detain food (for up to 21 days) which fails to comply with food safety requirements or which is likely to cause food poisoning or a foodborne disease. Food which is seized has to be dealt with by a Justice of the Peace. Any person liable to be prosecuted in respect of such food is entitled to make representations to the Justice of the Peace. If the food is not condemned, or detained food is cleared, compensation can be claimed. Any expenses incurred in the destruction of condemned food must be paid by the owner of the food.

Section 14. It is an offence to sell, to the prejudice of the purchaser, any food which is not of the nature (different kind or variety) or substance (not containing proper ingredients) or quality (inferior, for example, stale bread) demanded by the purchaser.

Section 15. It is an offence to sell, display or have in possession for the purpose of sale, food that is falsely described or labelled, which is misleading as to the nature or substance or quality.

Section 20. Enables proceedings to be taken against another person when the offence was due to his act or default.

Section 21. It is a defence for a person to prove that he took all reasonable precautions and exercised all due diligence to avoid the commission of the offence, by himself or by a person under his control.

Section 35. The penalty for most offences is:
- on conviction on indictment to an unlimited fine and/or up to two years' imprisonment;
- on summary conviction to a fine not exceeding the relevant amount and/or imprisonment for up to six months. (In the case of Sections 7, 8 or 14 the relevant amount is £20,000; the amount for the other sections is £5,000).

Section 40. This section empowers ministers to issue codes of practice to guide food authorities on the enforcement of food safety legislation. This is intended to assist in uniform standards of enforcement. The codes of practice are not legally binding but food authorities must have regard to them.

Statutory codes of practice

Section 40 of the Food Safety Act 1990, Regulation 24 of the Food Hygiene

Regulations 2006 and Regulation 6 of the official Feed and Food Controls Regulations 2006 permit ministers to issue codes of practice for enforcing authorities regarding the execution and enforcement of food law.

Currently there is one Food Law Code of Practice to which enforcement authorities must have regard when discharging their duties. There is also additional advice provided in a Food Law Practice Guidance to which enforcement officers may wish to adhere.

National guides to good hygiene practice

These guides provide food businesses with practical advice on complying with food safety regulations and must be given due consideration by enforcers. They will also assist in achieving consistency of enforcement. Guides are produced by trade associations and representatives of the specific industry but must be approved by the Food Standards Agency. The guides may be used in courts to illustrate good practice. However, food businesses do not have to follow the advice in any guide as they may wish to comply with the regulations in some other way.

Examples of guides include catering, retail baking and vending.

The Food Labelling Regulations, 1996

These regulations apply in England, Scotland and Wales and require most food sold for human consumption to be labelled with:
- the name of the food;
- a list of ingredients;
- a 'best-before' date which provides an indication of minimum durability (shelf life) or in the case of food which, microbiologically, is highly perishable and in consequence likely, after a short period, to constitute an immediate danger to human health, a 'use-by' date;
- any special storage conditions or conditions of use; and
- the name and address of the manufacturer, packer or seller.

The enforcement of food safety legislation in the United Kingdom

In the United Kingdom, central government has given the responsibility for protecting public health and ensuring food businesses comply with food hygiene legislation to local authorities. Authorized officers with a wide range of qualifications, experience and expertise are employed to enable authorities to carry out the significant range of food hygiene and food safety controls that now exist. The most common local authority official involved in food hygiene control is an environmental health practitioner (EHP)(Environmental Health Officer (EHO) in Scotland). Authorities may also appoint technical officers with specialist food qualifications. These officers are authorized to enforce the various acts and regulations.

The functions of authorized officers include:
- ensuring product safety and fitness for consumption;
- reducing possible sources of contamination entering the food environment;
- monitoring conditions and hygienic operations within the food environment;

- ensuring compliance with relevant legislation;
- establishing the integrity of management and effectiveness of control procedures; and
- offering professional guidance, including preventive advice, particularly when legislation is changing.

EHPs/EHOs undertake the above functions:
- during routine visits to and inspections of food premises;
- whilst investigating food poisoning outbreaks and incidents;
- whilst investigating food complaints;
- by lecturing on hygiene courses and seminars and giving related talks;
- by using the media, for example, press releases, committee reports and hazard warnings;
- whilst dealing with planning and licence applications;
- by developing partnerships with business's decision-making bases in the local authority's area (often referred to as the 'Home Authority Principle'); and
- by developing local business forums for the exchange of information and the provision of advice.

Inspections of food premises by authorized officers

Officers have the right to enter a food premises at any reasonable time, without notice. This means whenever there is activity at the business even if it is not open to the public.

Food hygiene inspections have two main purposes:
- to identify risks arising from the food business's activities and determine the effectiveness of the business's own assessment of hazards and controls; and
- to identify contraventions of food legislation and seek to have them corrected.

Before carrying out a food hygiene inspection, EHPs/EHOs will take account of a number of issues. These will include:
- reviewing the premises' history – including information on operations and systems, previous complaints and responses to earlier inspection outcomes;
- timing of inspection – generally unannounced, although advance notice may occasionally be appropriate to ensure relevant persons are present;
- equipment availability, for example, calibrated temperature recording equipment;
- appropriate protective clothing; and
- assessing the need for additional expertise, for example, food examiners.

Frequency of inspections

Effective inspection programmes recognize that the frequency of inspection will vary according to the type of food business, the nature of the food, the degree of handling and the size of the business. The frequency of visits is determined by the hazards associated with the business, including the current level of compliance with food safety legislation, the confidence of the enforcement officer in management, the history of compliance and the control systems in place. Essentially, those premises posing potentially a higher risk should be inspected more frequently than those premises with a lower risk. Businesses handling low-risk foods, with few customers, that comply with food hygiene legislation and are managed effectively may only be inspected every five years. Businesses processing high-risk food or at risk from *E coli* O157 or *Clostridium botulinum*, or supplying vulnerable consumers, are likely to be inspected at least every six months.

Action taken as a result of an inspection

During an inspection, an EHP/EHO may identify contraventions of food hygiene legislation and/or poor or unsafe food handling practices. Several options exist to remedy the contraventions and detailed guidance is found in the Food Law, Code of Practice as to the most appropriate action. The options available and potential outcomes for all food hygiene inspections include:

Informal action

Verbal or written advice/warnings where the EHP/EHO is confident the work will be carried out. Letters should clearly differentiate between legal requirements and recommendations. Information leaflets or posters may be provided and instruction or training could be given.

Formal action

A hygiene improvement notice, for contraventions of food hygiene legislation, allowing not less than 14 days to comply, for example, a cracked wash-hand basin or premises/equipment in disrepair. It would not be used for cleaning or anything that needs to be completed in less than 14 days;

The detention or seizure of unsafe food where food does not comply with the food safety requirements, for example, food which is unfit, responsible for causing food poisoning or contaminated with rat droppings. The food would be taken to a magistrate who has the power to condemn the food. The food business operator would probably be prosecuted. Alternatively the unfit food could be voluntarily surrendered to the authorized officer;

A hygiene emergency prohibition notice, where there is an imminent risk of injury to health, requiring closure of the premises or prohibition of processes or use of equipment (a court will issue a prohibition order if the proprietor is convicted and there is a risk of injury to health), for example, a serious pest infestation, sewage/flooding because of a drainage problem, no water, responsible for a food poisoning outbreak, too many ill staff, or no electricity. (These are also instances when a food business should voluntarily cease to trade);

A formal caution where an offence exists but it is not considered in the public interest to prosecute through the courts; and

Prosecution, where it is considered in the public interest. In order to take a successful prosecution, appropriate evidence will be required. Evidence can include, the notes taken at the time of inspection, photographs, witness statements and seized records, documents, equipment or food. The results of the laboratory tests regarding, for example, the seized food or swabs of work surfaces could also be used as evidence.

The defence of 'due diligence', in the Food Hygiene Regulations 2006 and the Food Safety Act 1990 is of specific note. The legislation creates a number of offences known as 'strict liability'. It does not matter that the accused did not intend to break the law. The mere fact that there is clear evidence that the statute has been contravened is sufficient for a conviction. This regime of strict liability was perceived as causing injustice if a person was held to have committed an offence for which he had no responsibility, or because of an accident or some cause completely beyond his control. To create a balance of fairness, the defence of 'due diligence' was included. The legislation specifically states that it is a defence to prove that all reasonable precautions were taken and all due diligence exercised to avoid the offence. Through legal precedent, various principles have been confirmed as necessary if a defence is to succeed. Some positive steps will always be required. Taking reasonable precautions involves the setting up of a system of control having regard to the nature of the risks involved. Due diligence involves securing the proper operation of that system. Where there is a reasonable precaution then it should be taken. Written records are not a legal requirement; however, satisfactory records may be useful to assist a due-diligence defence.

The Food Standards Agency

The Food Standards Agency was established on 1st April 2000. Its role is 'to protect public health from risks which may arise in connection with the consumption of food and otherwise to protect the interest of consumers in relation to food'.

The core values of the Agency are to:
- put the consumer first;
- be open and accessible; and
- be an independent voice.

The Agency's functions are to:
- provide advice and information to the public and to the government on food safety from farm to fork, nutrition and diet;
- protect consumers through effective enforcement and monitoring; and
- support consumer choice through promoting accurate and meaningful labelling.

The Food Standards Agency is led by a board and accounts to Parliament through Health Ministers. The headquarters are based in London. Scottish, Welsh and Northern Irish Executives of the Agency are responsible for implementing policies on food issues specific to each country within the Agency's framework.

The Agency has responsibility for:
- food safety, contaminants, nutrition, additives and labelling;
- animal feed and veterinary public health;
- the performance of Local Authority enforcement;
- the Meat Hygiene Service; and
- research.

Website: www.foodstandards.gov.uk

SUPERVISING FOOD SAFETY (LEVEL 3) Glossary

Glossary

Acute disease	A disease which develops rapidly and produces symptoms quickly after infection. Patients soon recover, or die.
Additive	A chemical added to food, e.g. a preservative, a colouring or flavouring agent.
Aerobic	Using oxygen.
Aerobic colony count	The count of viable aerobic bacteria per gram of product (based on the number of colonies grown on nutrient agar plate).
Algae	Simple plants capable of photosynthesis and most commonly found in aquatic environments or damp soil, for example, seaweed and spirogyra (forms bright green slimy masses in ponds).
Allergen	Any substance, usually a protein, which is capable of inducing an allergy.
Allergy	An identifiable immunological response to food or food additives, which may involve the respiratory system, the gastrointestinal tract, the skin or the central nervous system. In severe cases this may result in anaphylactic shock.
Ambient temperature	The temperature of the surroundings. Usually refers to the room temperature.
Anaerobic	Using little or no oxygen.
Antibiotic	A drug used to destroy pathogenic bacteria within human or animal bodies.
Antiseptic	A substance that prevents the growth of bacteria and moulds, specifically on or in the human body.
Aseptic	Free from micro-organisms.
A_W (water activity)	A measure of the water available to micro-organisms in food.
Bactericide	A substance which destroys bacteria.
Binary fission	Asexual method of reproduction by the division of the nucleus into two daughter nuclei, followed by similar division of the cell body. The method of reproduction used by bacteria.
Biodegradable	Chemicals and materials which can be broken down by bacteria or other biological means (usually during sewage treatment).
Carrier	A person who harbours, and may transmit, pathogenic organisms without showing signs of illness.
Chronic disease	A disease which usually develops slowly and symptoms last for a prolonged period.
Chronic poison	A substance which is used at low concentration and relies on repeated intake by the target pest to ensure elimination.
Cleaning	The process of removing soil, food residues, dirt, grease and other objectionable matter.
Clean-in-place	The process of cleaning equipment and machinery whilst it is in situ and assembled. It usually involves circulating strong detergents and disinfectants at high temperatures through pipework and equipment in factories.
Clean surface	A surface which is free from residual film or soil, has no objectionable odour, is not greasy to touch and will not discolour a white paper tissue wiped over it.
Competent authority	The central authority of a member state competent to ensure compliance with relevant regulations, or any other authority to which that central authority has delegated that competence.
Contact time	The period of time required by a cleaning chemical, such as a disinfectant, to be effective and achieve its objective, i.e. to reduce bacteria to a safe level.
Contamination	The presence or introduction of a hazard. (EC Regulation No. 852/2004)
Controlled atmosphere packing	The packaging of food in an atmosphere that is different from the normal composition of air, the gases being precisely adjusted to specific concentration which are maintained throughout storage.

SUPERVISING FOOD SAFETY (LEVEL 3) Glossary

Critical control point (CCP)	A step in the process at which control can be applied and is essential to prevent or eliminate a food safety hazard or reduce it to an acceptable level.
Cross-contamination	The transfer of bacteria from contaminated food (usually raw) to ready-to-eat foods by direct contact, drip or indirect contact using a vehicle such as the hands or a cloth.
Danger zone of bacterial growth	The temperature range within which the multiplication of most pathogenic bacteria is possible, i.e. from 5°C to 63°C. Most rapid growth takes place between 20°C and 50°C.
Dehydrate	To remove water.
Detergent	A chemical that facilitates the removal of grease and food particles and promotes cleanliness.
Disinfectant	A chemical used for disinfection.
Disinfection	The reduction of micro-organisms to a safe level. The term disinfection normally refers to the treatment of premises, surfaces and equipment, but may also be applied to the treatment of skin.
Epidemiology	The study of disease of people and animals, including incidence, sources, causes, mode of spread, distribution and controls.
First-aid materials	Suitable and sufficient bandages and dressings, including water-proof dressings and antiseptic.
Foodborne disease	An illness resulting from the consumption of food (or water) contaminated by pathogenic micro-organisms (and/or toxins) which do not need to multiply within the food to cause illness.
Food business	Means any undertaking, whether for profit or not, and whether public or private, carrying out any of the activities related to any stage of production, processing and distribution of food.
Food handling	Any operation in the production, preparation, processing, packaging, storage, transport, distribution and sale of food.
Food hygiene	The measures and conditions necessary to control hazards and to ensure fitness for human consumption of a foodstuff taking into account its intended use. (EC Regulation No. 852/2004)
Food pest	An animal which lives in or on our food. It contaminates the food and is destructive, noxious or troublesome.
Food poisoning	An acute illness of sudden onset caused by the recent consumption of contaminated or poisonous food.
Fungi	Plants unable to synthesize their own food and usually parasitic or saprophytic. Include single-celled microscopic yeasts, moulds, mildews and toadstools.
Fungicide	A substance that kills fungi and mould.
Galvanized metal	Iron or steel which has been coated with zinc for protection against corrosion.
Gastroenteritis	An inflammation of the stomach and intestinal tract that normally results in diarrhoea.
Grease trap	A device fitted into a drainage system to prevent fat and grease entering the sewer.
Hazard	A biological, chemical or physical agent in, or condition of, food with the potential to cause harm (an adverse health effect) to the consumer. (NB most biological hazards are microbiological.)
High-risk foods	Ready-to-eat foods which, under favourable conditions, support the multiplication of pathogenic bacteria and are intended for consumption without treatment which would destroy such organisms.

SUPERVISING FOOD SAFETY (LEVEL 3) Glossary

Immunity	The ability to resist an invading organism so that the body does not develop the disease.
Incubation period	The period between infection (or ingestion) and the first signs of illness.
Infective dose	The number of a particular micro-organism required under normal circumstances to produce clinical signs of a disease.
Moulds	Microscopic plants (fungi) that may appear as woolly patches on food.
Mycotoxin	A toxin produced by some moulds.
Neurotoxin	A toxin that affects the nervous system.
Onset period	The period between consumption of the food and the first signs of illness (where incubation of micro-organisms within the body does not take place).
Optimum	Best.
Pasteurization	A heat process used to reduce the number of micro-organisms to a safe level. Pasteurized food must be stored under refrigeration.
Pathogen	Disease-producing organism.
Pesticide	A chemical used to kill pests.
pH	An index used as a measure of acidity or alkalinity.
Potable water	Water meeting the minimum requirements laid down in Council Directive 98/83/EC of 3 November 1998 on the quality of water intended for human consumption.
Primary production	Those stages in the food chain up to and including, for example, harvesting, slaughtering, milking and fishing.
Protozoa	Single-celled organisms which form the basis of the food chain. Some are pathogenic, e.g. cryptosporidium.
Quats	A popular name for quaternary ammonium compounds.
Residual insecticide	A long-lasting insecticide applied in such a way that it remains active for a considerable period of time.
Risk	The likelihood of a hazard occurring in food.
Risk assessment	The process of identifying hazards, assessing risks and evaluating their significance.
Safe food	Food which is free of contaminants and will not cause illness, harm or injury.
Sanitizer	A chemical agent used for cleansing and disinfecting surfaces and equipment.
Spore	A resistant resting-phase of bacteria which protects them against adverse conditions.
Sterile	Free from all living organisms.
Sterilization	A process that destroys all micro-organisms, toxins and spores.
Total viable count	The total number of living cells detectable in a sample. The number of cells is assessed from the number of colonies which develop on incubation of a suitable medium which has been inoculated with the sample of bacteria.
Toxins	Poisons produced by pathogens.
Viruses	Microscopic pathogens that multiply in living cells of their host.
Yeast	A single-celled fungus which reproduces by budding and grows rapidly on certain foodstuffs, especially those containing sugar. Yeasts are the chief agents of fermentation. (Sugar converted to alcohol and carbon dioxide.)
Zoonoses	Diseases which can pass from animal to man and vice versa.

Index

A

Accelerated freeze drying, 73
Acetic acid, 74
Acid fermentation, 68, 74
Acid foods, 5, 10, 35, 52, 71
Acidification, 74
Acute disease, 150
Additive, 150
Adenosine triphosphate (ATP), 96
Aerobes, 10, 67, 74
Aerobic, 150
Aerobic colony count, 150
Aerosol fly spray, 104
Air-blast freezing, 69
Alcohols, 92
Algae, 150
Allergen, 23-25, 150
Allergenic hazards, 23
Allergy, 150
Alpha-amylase test, 70
Alphachloralose, 105
Ambient temperature, 150
Anaerobes, 10, 67, 74
Anaerobic, 150
Anaphylaxis, 23, 25
Antibiotics, 74, 150
Antimony, 35
Antiseptic, 150
Aprons, 47
Aquatic biotoxins, 36
Artificial drying, 72
Aseptic, 150
Authorized officer, 116, 130, 132-134, 141-143, 145-147
Autolytic enzymes, 67
A$_W$, 150

B

Bacillary dysentery, 37, 41
Bacillus cereus, 11, 30, 40
Bacteria, 8, 9, 14, 15, 27
Bacterial contamination, 14, 15
Bacterial multiplication, 9, 10
Bactericide, 150
Bacteriological monitoring, 127
Bacteriology, 8
Bains-marie, 66
Bait boxes, 22, 103, 104
Bakery products, 12
Benefits of high standards of hygiene, 5
Benzene, 34
Best-before date, 54, 133
Binary fission, 9, 150
Biodegradable, 150
Biological hazards, 125
Bird pests, 102
Bivalves, 6, 36
Blanching, 69, 72
Blast chillers, 59
Blast-freezing, 65
Bleach, 12, 92
Blowflies, 100
Boils, 8, 45, 49
Bolts, 19
Booklice, 101
Botulinum cook, 71
Botulism outbreak, 34
Brining, 73
Bristles, 21, 91
Brown Rat, 99
Brushes, 85, 91
Building design, 19, 77, 102

C

Cadmium, 35
Calcium proprionate, 74
Campylobacter, 38, 43
Campylobacter jejuni, 38, 41
Canned foods, 6, 15, 52, 71
Canning, 71
Caramelization, 70
Carriers, 6, 15, 16, 37, 44, 48, 119, 140, 150
Causal factors, 32
Causative agent, 27
Caustic soda, 90
Ceilings, 77
Cell membrane, 9
Cell wall, 9, 11
Cereals, 52
Chemical additives, 34
Chemical control methods, 104
Chemical disinfection, 92
Chemical energy, 90
Chemical food poisoning, 34
Chemical hazards, 14, 23, 126
Chemical preservation, 73
Chemical store, 89
Chill holding, 144
Chlorinated water, 72
Chronic disease, 150
Chronic poison, 150
Chopping boards, 87
Cleaning, 89-97, 150
   activities, 21
   benefits, 89
   chemicals, 23
   energy, 90
   equipment, 91, 93
   facilities, 80

SUPERVISING FOOD SAFETY (LEVEL 3) Index

of equipment, 86
problems, 89
procedures, 93
schedules, 96
Clean-in-place, 150
Clean surface, 150
Cling film, 53
Cloakrooms, 81
Clostridium botulinum, 11, 31, 34, 40, 71, 72, 75, 148
Clostridium perfringens, 10, 11, 28, 34, 40, 74
Cloths, 15, 22, 91, 93
Cocci, 8
Cockroaches, 100
Codes, 54
Codes of Practice, 142, 145
Codex Alimentarius, 122, 123
Coeliacs, 24
Colonies, 8
Colour coding, 16, 54, 86, 91
Coloured waterproof dressing, 45
Commensals, 8
Commercially sterile, 70. 71
Compactors, 82
Competent authority, 150
Competition, 11
Condemned food, 145
Condensation, 19, 51, 54, 79, 94, 124
Construction of equipment, 83
Construction of premises, 77
Consultant in communicable disease control, 121
Contact time, 89, 90, 92, 150
Containers, 18
Contamination, 14, 17, 63, 87, 150
Contamination control, 16

Controlled atmosphere packing, 74, 150
Controlled atmospheres, 74
Control measures, 18, 28-32, 37-39, 122, 126, 131-133
Convalescent carriers, 6
Cook-chill, 55, 64-65
Cooked meat slicing machine (cleaning of), 95
Cook-freeze, 65
Cooking, 10, 11, 58, 70
CookSafe, 134
Cooling, 59, 140
Copper, 35
Corrective action, 122, 128, 131-133
Cost of poor hygiene, 4
Craft knives, 15
Cream, 52
Criminal Justice Act, 1991, 143
Critical control point, 122, 126, 151
Critical limit, 122, 126, 131-133
Cross-contamination, 15, 38, 87, 151
Cryogenic freezing, 69
Curing, 73
Customer complaints, 12, 17, 113
Customer contamination, 22
Cut-out switches, 78
Cuts, 45, 49
Cytoplasm, 9

D
Damaged stock, 53
Danger zone of bacterial growth, 151
Data loggers, 58
De-boxing, 76

Decision tree, 122
Dehydrate, 151
Dehydration, 10, 51, 72
Deliveries, 16, 50, 61
Dental sepsis, 49
Design of premises, 76, 136
Destruction of bacteria, 11
Detergents, 90, 151
Deviation, 122
Diarrhetic shellfish poisoning, 36
Diffusers, 20
Digital probe thermometers, 157
Disinfectant, 12, 92, 151
Disinfection, 80, 91, 151
Disinfection frequency, 93
Distribution, 4, 61
Documentation, 129
Doors, 77
Drainage, 79
Drip, 15, 56
Drivers, 16
Dry-goods stores, 54
Due diligence, 18, 22, 105, 112, 119, 126, 130, 132, 135, 142, 145, 148
Duration of illness, 28-31, 36, 38-42
Dustbins, 81
Dysentery, 37

E
Ears, 45, 49
Eggs, 51
Electrical supplies, 78
Electronic fly killers, 21, 22, 104
Endotoxins, 10
End product testing, 122
Enforcement, 146
Engineers, 19, 21

SUPERVISING FOOD SAFETY (LEVEL 3) Index

Enteric fever, 37
Enterotoxins, 11
Environmental control, 102
Environmental Health Department, 48, 53, 62
Environmental health practitioner/officer, 119, 120, 133-134, 146-147,
Enzymes, 61, 62, 67, 68, 69, 75
Epidemiology, 151
Equipment, 83, 139
Equipment design, 83-86
Escherichia coli O157, 39, 41, 44, 148
European Union, 135
Exclusion of food handlers, 43, 48, 140
Exotoxins, 10, 11
Extraneous matter, 17, 18

F

Facultative anaerobes, 10
Faecal-oral route, 36, 37, 39, 43
Faecal specimens, 120
Failure of management, 33
False ceilings, 102
Fermentation, 74
Fingernails, 44
First aid, 46, 151
Flagella, 9
Flaking paint, 19
Flexible connections, 78
Flies, 100
Floors, 78
Flour, 52
Flow diagram, 122, 125
Fluctuating temperatures, 62
Fluidized-bed freezing, 69
Foodborne disease, 36-42, 151
Food business, 151

Food handlers, 21, 43-49, 117
Food handling, 151
Food hygiene, 4, 151
Food Hygiene (England) (Wales) (Scotland) (NI) Regs. 2006, 135, 141
Food hygiene inspections, 147
Food Labelling Regs.1996, 146
Food pest, 152
Food poisoning, 4, 6, 7, 8, 9, 27-36, 151
Food poisoning bacteria, 9, 10, 25 27-34
Food poisoning outbreaks, 32, 33, 119
Food premises, 76-83, 136
Food preparation, 60
Food preservation, 68
Food rooms, 137
Food Safety Act 1990, 143, 145
Food safety hazards, 125
Food safety management system, 122, 136
Food safety policies, 112
Food safety requirements, 136
Food service, 60
Food Standards Agency, 149
Foodstuffs, 140
Food vehicles, 15, 16, 27, 28-32, 39, 119
Food waste, 81, 139
Footwear, 48, 81
Foreign bodies, 14, 17, 18, 126
Foreign body detection, 22
Formal caution, 141
Freezer breakdown, 62
Freezer burn, 62, 67, 69
Freezing, 12, 62
Freezing systems, 69
Frozen food, storage of, 61

Frozen poultry, 63
Fruit, 51
Fruit Flies, 100
Fumigation, 105
Fungi, 12, 151
Fungicide, 34, 151

G

Galvanised metal, 35, 151
Gas supplies, 78
Gastroenteritis, 6, 36, 151
Gelatin, 144
Generation time, 9
Generic controls, 32
German Cockroach, 101
Glass, 20
Good housekeeping, 103
Good hygiene practice, 112, 124
Grease, 19,
Grease trap, 79, 151
Greenhouse effect, 53
Growth curve, 10

H

HACCP, 18, 64, 122-134
HACCP based systems, 134
HACCP control chart, 131-133
HACCP plan, 130
HACCP principles, 122, 123, 125-130, 136
HACCP team, 122
Haemolytic uraemic syndrome, 39
Hair, 46
Hairnets, 46
Hand-contact surfaces, 16
Hand disinfection, 93
Hand drying, 44
Hands, 44
Handwashing, 44
Handwashing facilities, 80

Haricot beans, 35
Hazard analysis, 122, 125
Hazards, 14, 18, 33, 43, 46, 65, 122, 125, 131-133, 151
Health Protection Agency, 121
Health Protection Scotland, 121
Healthy carriers, 6
Heat disinfection, 92
Heat resistant bacteria, 69, 70, 71
Heat treatment, 140
Hepatitis A, 39, 41
High-risk food, 5, 8, 56, 61, 148, 151
Home authority principle, 147
Hot cupboards, 66
Hot food, 56, 144
Hot holding, 66, 144
Hot plates, 66
House Mouse, 99
Hydrogen gas, 35
Hygiene emergency prohibition notice/order, 142
Hygiene improvement notice, 141
Hygiene prohibition order, 141, 142
Hygiene regulations, 141
Hygiene training, 117-119
Hypochlorite, 94

I
Ice cream, 49
Ice crystals, 62, 63, 69
Immunity, 151
Incidence of food poisoning, 7
Incubation period, 27-31, 36-39, 152
Induction training, 117
Infective dose, 36, 39, 152
Infestation, signs of, 99, 101
Infested food, 21

Infrared thermometer, 58
Injurious to health, 145
Insects, 21, 67, 100
Inspection belt, 18
Inspection of food premises, 114-117, 147
Investigation of food poisoning, 119
Irradiation, 12, 75, 91
ISO 9000, 111, 114

J
Jewellery, 20, 46
Justice of the Peace, 143, 145

K
Kinetic energy, 90
Kitchen design, 82, 84

L
Lactic acid, 74
Lacto bacillus, 70
Lead, 35
Lighting, 80
Lipases, 68
Liquid egg, 70
Liquid soap, 44, 93
Listeria monocytogenes, 38, 41
Listeriosis, 38
Load-line, 57, 61
Lockers, 81
Low-acid canned foods, 70
Low-acid foods, 71
Low-dose pathogens, 35
Low-risk food, 5, 147

M
Main clean, 93
Maintenance operatives, 21
Management failures, 33

Manual dish washing, 94
Market stalls, 138
Meat pies, 51
Mechanical dishwashing, 94
Mechanical equipment, 91
Medical questionnaire, 48
Mesophiles, 10
Metallic food poisoning, 35
Microbiological contamination, 14
Microbiological hazards, 125
Microbiology, 8
Micro-organisms, 8
Milk, 52, 70
Modified atmosphere packaging, 74
Modified atmosphere packs, 53
Monitoring, 57, 123, 126
Monitoring food handlers, 128
Monitoring records, 129-130
Monitoring temperatures, 57
Motivation, 113
Mould inhibitors, 12
Moulds, 12, 14, 51, 52, 67, 69, 152
Mouldy food, 14
Mouth, 8, 45
Multi-deck units, 55
Mussels, 35
Mycelium, 12
Mycotoxins, 67, 152

N
Nail-biters, 45
Nailbrushes, 44
Nail varnish, 45
Narcotizing, 105
NASA, 122
National Guides to Good Practice, 136, 146
Negligent cleaning, 89
Neurotoxin, 152

SUPERVISING FOOD SAFETY (LEVEL 3) Index

Nisin, 74
Nitrates and nitrites, 73
Non-potable water, 79
Norovirus, 36, 42
Norway Rat, 99
Nose, 8, 45
Notice boards, 20
Nuclear material, 9
Nutrients, 9
Nuts, 19, 21

O
Obstruction, 143
Oil, 19, 20, 82
Olive oil, 35
Onset period, 27-31, 35, 36, 38-42
Optimum, 9, 152
Optimum temperature, 10, 90
Organoleptic assessment, 127
Oriental Cockroach, 100
Outbreak control team, 119
Outbreak location, 119
Out-of-date, 16, 56
Overloading of refrigerators, 56
Oxygen, 10, 67, 68, 74
Oysters, 5, 6, 35

P
Packaging, 18, 19, 50, 53, 62, 70, 76, 103, 112, 140
Packing, 18, 56
Paper sacks, 19
Paper towels, 21, 44, 94
Paralytic shellfish poisoning, 36
Parasites, 39, 67, 69, 75
Paratyphoid, 37, 42
Pasteurization, 70, 152
Pasteurized canned foods, 72
Pasties, 51
Pathogens, 8, 74, 98, 100, 144, 152

Penalties, 143, 145
Perfume, 46
Perimeter areas, 82
Perishable food, 57
Personal hygiene, 43-49, 140
Person-to-person spread, 36, 39
Pest control, 22, 98, 102
Pest control contractor, 105
Pesticide, 34, 35, 152
pH, 10, 67, 71, 73, 74, 112, 152
Pharoah's Ants, 101
Physical contamination, 14, 17
Physical control methods, 104
Physical hazards, 18, 126
Pickling, 74
Pillsbury Company, 122
Plate freezing, 69
Poisonous fish, 35
Poisonous plankton, 36
Poisonous plants, 35
Polypropylene, 85, 87, 91, 94
Potable water, 152
Power of entry, 142
Pre-clean, 93
Prejudice of the purchaser, 145
Premises, 131
Preparation surfaces, 86
Prerequisites programmes, 123, 124
Preservation, 68-75
Preservatives, 67, 73-74
Prevention of contamination, 15
Price tickets, 55
Primary production, 152
Principles of HACCP, 122, 125-130, 136
Proofing of buildings, 102
Propionates, 74
Protective clothing, 47, 140
Protozoa, 13, 152

Psocids, 101
Psoriasis, 49
Psychrophiles, 10
Public Health Laboratory Service, 121
Puffer fish, 35
Purulent gingivitis, 49

Q
Quality assurance, 113
Quality control, 114
Quaternary ammonium compounds, 92
Quats, 152

R
Radiant heat, 57
Rancidity, 61, 68, 69, 74, 75
Rats, 99
Raw foods, 6, 50, 144
Raw materials, 17, 18, 19, 50, 71, 112, 140
Raw meat, 50
Raw poultry, 6, 38, 50
Ready-to-eat raw foods, 6
Reasonable precautions, 22
Red kidney beans, 35
Red whelk poisoning, 35
Refresher training, 118
Refrigerators, 55-57, 68
Refuse, 76, 81, 139
Regeneration, 64, 65
Registration, 136
Regulation (EC) No. 852/2004, 136
Reheating, 65, 144
Report, 116
Reservoir, 39
Residual insecticide, 152
Review of HACCP, 129

157

SUPERVISING FOOD SAFETY (LEVEL 3) Index

Rhubarb leaves, 35
Rinse aid, 95
Risk, 123, 152
Risk groups, 7
Risk assessment, 152
Rodenticides, 104
Rodents, 21, 99
Rods, 8
Roller drying, 72
Rope, 68
Routes, 15, 16
Rust, 19

S
Safe food, 4, 152
Safer food, better business, 134
Salmonella, 7, 27, 33, 40, 98, 101
Salmonella Paratyphi, 37, 42
Salmonella Typhi, 37, 42
Salt, 73
Samples of food, 142
Sanitary conveniences, 81
Sanitizer, 91, 152
Satellite kitchens, 64
Sausage rolls, 51
Scientific assessment, 144
Scombrotoxic fish poisoning, 35
Seams, 72
Seizure, 145, 148
Septic spots, 45
Services, 78
Sewage, 15, 27, 36, 37, 38
Shelf life, 50, 55, 70, 74, 144
Shellfish, 5, 36, 39
Shellfish poisoning, 36
Shigella sonnei, 37, 41, 44
Sinks, 80
Site selection, 76
Siting of equipment, 86

Skin infections, 8, 43, 45, 49
Slicing machine, cleaning of, 95
Smoking, 46, 75
Sodium nitrate, 35, 73
Sodium nitrite, 35, 73
Sodium proprionate, 74
Specifications, 18, 112
Specimens (faecal), 120
Spillages, 57, 103
Spirochaetes, 8
Spoilage, 8, 10, 49, 53, 61, 67-68, 75
Spores, 11, 12, 29, 30, 31, 58, 67, 69, 70, 72, 73, 75, 91, 152
Spray drying, 72
Staff responsibilities (refrigerators), 57
Staff training, 117
Staleness, 68
Standards, 111
Staphylococcus, 8, 73
Staphylococcus aureus, 29, 33, 40, 43, 45
Staples, 18
Steam, 12, 70, 79
Steam disinfection, 92
Sterile, 152
Sterilization, 70, 92, 152
Sterilizing sinks, 80
Sterilizing units, 92
Sticky fly papers, 104
Stock control, 54, 56, 62
Stock rotation, 54, 56, 62
Storage times (frozen food), 62
Stored product insects, 101
String, 18, 21
Sugar, 73
Sulphur dioxide, 74
Sun drying, 72

Supervisor, role of, 120
Supervisory management, 111-134
Suppliers, 18, 19, 112
Supply of Machinery (Safety) Regs.1992, 85
Symptoms, 27-31, 34-42

T
Taenia saginata, 39
Taint, 23, 46, 50, 51, 67
Tapeworms, 39
Target level, 123
Thawing, 61, 62, 63, 64
Thermal energy, 90
Thermometer, 57, 58, 61, 64
Thermophiles, 10
Tin, 35
Tobacco, 46
Tolerance, 123
Total viable count, 152
Toxins, 6, 10, 12, 27, 35, 58, 65, 69, 70, 75, 144, 152
Training, 43, 112, 117-119, 141
Training methods, 118
Training programme, 118
Training records, 118
Transport, 139
Typhoid, 37, 42

U
Ultra heat treatment, 70
Unfit food, 10, 12, 16, 21, 50, 53, 54
Unloading, 50
Unpacking, 18
Use-by-date, 12, 53, 54, 146

V

Vacuum packs, 12, 15, 53, 69, 74
Validation, 123
Vegetables, 6, 51, 54, 57, 62, 67, 69, 71, 72
Vegetative bacteria, 11, 12
Vegetative state, 9
Vehicles, 9, 15, 16, 31
Ventilation, 79
Vericleen, 93, 97
Verification, 123, 129
  of effective training, 119
Vibrios, 8
Viral gastroenteritis, 36
Viruses, 13, 14, 15, 27, 36, 152
Visitors, 113

W

Walls, 77
Washing facilities, 80
Wasps, 100
Waste disposal systems, 81
Waste food, 76, 81, 139
Water supply, 78, 139
Waterproof conduits, 78
Waterproof dressings, 55
Weedkillers, 34
Weil's disease, 98
Windows, 77
Wood splinters, 19
Workflow, 76
Wrapping, 53, 140

Y

Yeasts, 12, 13, 67, 69, 152

Z

Zinc, 35
Zoonoses, 152